To Dear Peter
Happy Christmas

We reckon you will be Moooooooved to tears

lots of love from

Sarah + Mich xx

Christmas 2011

BEAUTIFUL COWS

PORTRAITS

of

CHAMPION
BREEDS

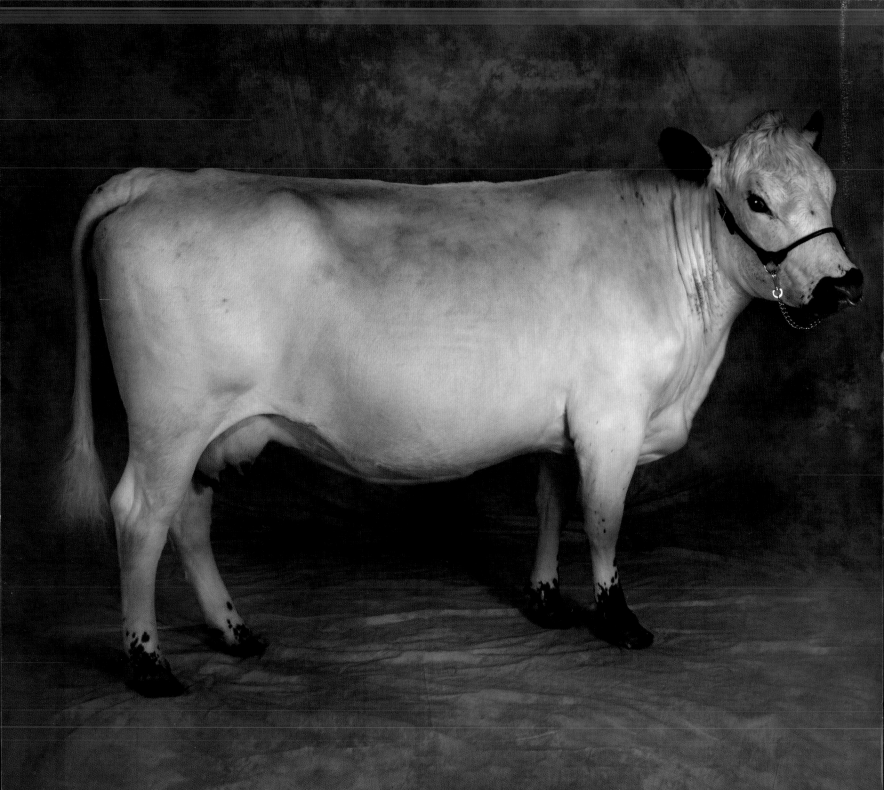

BEAUTIFUL COWS

PORTRAITS

of

CHAMPION
BREEDS

by VAL PORTER

photographed by
JEREMY HOPLEY *&* ANDREW PERRIS

FRANCES LINCOLN LIMITED
PUBLISHERS

Frances Lincoln Limited
4 Torriano Mews
Torriano Avenue
London NW5 2RZ
www.franceslincoln.com

British Library Cataloguing in Publication Data
A catalogue record for this book is available from the British Library

This book was conceived, designed, and produced by

Ivy Press
210 High street, Lewes, East Sussex, BN7 2NS, UK

Creative Director **Peter Bridgewater**
Publisher **Jason Hook**
Editorial Director **Tom Kitch**
Art Director **Wayne Blades**
Senior Editor **Polita Anderson**
Designer **Kate Haynes**
Photographers **Jeremy Hopley, Andrew Perris**
Photography Assistant **Josh New**
Illustrator **David Anstey**

ISBN: 978-0-7112-3081-1
First Edition: 2010
Printed in China

CONTENTS

INTRODUCTION

I T IS THE EYES THAT DRAW YOU IN: LARGE, PEACEFUL, gazing at nothing in particular. Cows are leisurely and amiable beasts, with time to stand and stare – though they might claim that really they are working hard at chewing the cud and ruminating about life.

The aim of *Beautiful Cows* is to capture their bovine beauty, their character and some of the many differences between the thousand or so breeds of cattle worldwide. They have been photographed looking their best, pampered for the show-ring at major shows in the UK and the US, where only the outstanding are on display.

Cows can be very beautiful, but their beauty is difficult to capture through the lens. They will stand placidly, even dreamily, for those they know – sometimes too dreamily, heads drooping too much for a good photo. In contrast they can be wary of strangers and then those eyes (positioned at the side of the head for good all-round vision) widen and roll with alarm, the tail begins to lift and the unsuspecting photographer is presented with a quantity of forcefully ejected brown liquid cowpat, disgracing the catwalk.

Above: It takes patience, determination and skill to photograph cows.

Each photograph in this book is accompanied by a page with information on the breed's history, qualities and appearance. A rough idea of body weights is given though this is only a broad indication: so much depends on the environment in which a cow finds herself.

The cows are presented more or less chronologically insofar as they became a 'proper' breed, starting with the oldest, more traditional ones and ending with those whose history is measured in mere decades. There are breeds that originated in Europe, others that were created on the American continent from a mixture of European and Asian cattle, and a representative of the huge variety of African cows as well. To some extent the selection has been determined by what was exhibited at the shows we attended, and a major gap to British eyes might be the splendid, rare WHITE PARK, one of the most ancient breeds in the UK but, for us, camera shy. The book is not intended to be a catalogue of breeds – it just gives a taste of some of them. We invite you to relax and enjoy the beauty of cows for their own sake.

COWS IN CIVILIZATION

THE WILD ANCESTOR OF DOMESTICATED COWS WAS the aurochs (*Bos primigenius*), a big beast that spread across Asia and North Africa (becoming extinct in both continents some 3,000 years ago) and Europe, but never reached America or Australasia. The last wild auroch in Europe, a lonely cow, was killed in a Polish forest in 1627. The aurochs had huge horns and European bulls were up to 1.8 m (6 ft) tall at the shoulder. Bulls had black coats, a pale stripe on the back, a topknot of curly white hairs on the head and a white ring around the muzzle. Cows were largely reddish.

Nearly all of the world's domesticated cows today are descended from the aurochs and domestication probably began around 8,500 years ago, in Eurasia. At first, all the domesticants had long horns like the aurochs. In some regions long horns were favoured; in others, especially in Europe (they reached central Europe about 5,000 years ago), the cattle were bred for shorter and shorter horns. From Europe short-horned cattle reached Egypt and spread towards Ethiopia and also along the northern coast into West Africa.

Above: Maiherpri greets the Divine Herd in *The Book of the Dead*, whose food offerings guarantee sustenance for Maiherpri in the Underworld.

Britain had plenty of wild aurochs when the island was still connected to Europe by a land bridge, but wild cattle had died out some 3,000 years earlier, during the Bronze Age. By the time domesticated cattle reached northern Europe, Britain was isolated, but domesticants were brought into the country by boat.

Cows proved to be enormously valuable animals in all cultures that raised them. They gave milk, meat, tallow for candles, hides for leather, horn for tools and lantern panes, muscle power for pulling carts and ploughing the fields, dung for manure or fuel, and so much more. Bulls sometimes had a rough time: they were sacrificed by the Druids, for example, and their propensity to charge made them the subject of 'sports' such as bull-jumping and bull-fighting in some cultures. But the generous bountiful cows were cared for and in several cultures were worshipped – especially in ancient Egypt, India and some parts of Africa. In contrast, they are grossly exploited in many modern Western agricultural systems, often to the point of inexcusable inhumanity.

THE DEVELOPMENT OF BREEDS

IN BRITAIN, LOCAL PREFERENCES FOR CERTAIN TYPES of cow gradually evolved, based on what would survive best in local conditions. For centuries herds were free to mingle on common land and breeding was haphazard. It was not until the 18th-century enclosures that farmers began to choose which bull should mate with which cow and why. At first they selected on the basis of the 'best' bull – usually one they just liked the look of. Some farmers preferred polled cattle – those genetically unable to grow horns. These were easier to handle and there was a superstition that the growing of horns misdirected the animal's energies away from producing more meat and milk.

Selective breeding was pioneered by the famous Leicestershire master breeder Robert Bakewell (1725–1795). Instead of bulls and cows mating at random, he acquired large rangy plate-footed OLD LONGHORN cows from many different sources in northern England, kept the sexes separate, chose the best combinations and then bred them deliberately 'in-and-in' (inbreeding to fix certain traits).

Above: There are roughly 240 known zebu breeds and varieties, found mostly in Africa, the Indian subcontinent and China.

A breed is a type carefully selected over time, that reliably reproduces its qualities and appearance in its offspring. It takes generations of dedicated selection to create and 'fix' a new breed, and some say that it is only a true breed if it has its own breed society, laying down very specific requirements about body conformation, coat colour and pattern, horns and so on. The emphasis on coat colour and pattern was taken to extremes during the 19th century, when breed societies first emerged.

While Britain and other European countries have been developing their cows into breeds for centuries (and likewise in Asia and Africa), America and Australasia had been isolated by oceans from the rest of the world. All of their domesticated cattle originally had to be shipped in, almost entirely from Europe, with the early explorers and settlers.

The first domesticated cattle to cross the Atlantic from Europe went with Columbus to the Caribbean islands at the end of the 15th century. The earliest cattle in Australia arrived with settlers in the First Fleet in 1788 and were Indian ZEBU acquired from the Cape.

THE BREEDS

THE MAIN ROLES FOR COWS ALL OVER THE WORLD are as draught animals (pulling anything from carts to ploughs), milk producers and for beef. Originally, most served all three roles and are therefore termed *triple-purpose*. With muscle power giving way to mechanisation, the 'draught' element faded out and the majority became *dual-purpose*: cows could give milk for the dairy and also raise their own sturdy calves for beef (in which case they are known as suckler cows). Increasingly, cows have become *single-purpose* specialists and today many are either dairy or beef breeds.

Dairy cows tend to be skinny, even bony, and wedge-shaped (narrower at the front, whether viewed from the side or above); they put their energy into making milk, not meat, and the breeder is more interested in a good udder and the ability to become pregnant regularly. *Suckler* cows have a chunkier look and are often cross-bred with even beefier bull breeds, as the emphasis is more on producing lots of good beef, usually cheaply on grazing rather than with artificial feeding on concentrates. Pure *beef* breeds are generally rectangular in shape and of course muscular. *Draught* breeds tend to carry their weight in the shoulders.

There is immense variation between breeds – not just in body shape and function but more obviously in the huge range of coat colours and patterns, and differences in the length and shape of the horns. In Africa, dramatically long horns have been favoured for millennia by many tribes; Africans have also proved superb masters in breeding for specific coat patterns, many not seen in European cattle; some of these were so precise that cow-hide shields were used to identify different tribes in battle.

Coat colours range from pure white to pure black, through shades of yellow, red and brown. Sometimes the colours are 'whole' or solid; often they are broken with patches (pied), streaks and speckles of other colours, especially white, or are a mingling of individual hairs of two colours (roan). Some breeds always have white faces, or white coats with coloured 'points' (ears, muzzles, tail switches), or coloured coats with a white belt around the waist.

Above: Despite many old wives' tales, colour does not necessarily indicate productive traits like quantity and quality of milk.

BREEDS AROUND THE WORLD

OWS ARE UNIVERSAL: THEY ARE SO ADAPTABLE that they are found in every continent and environment. Worldwide, the cattle population is heading for 1.4 billion animals, most of which are in India, Brazil and China, followed by the US, the EU, Argentina, Australia and Mexico. Within the EU, the top five beef and veal producers are France, Germany, Italy, the UK and Spain; the top five cows' milk producers are Germany, France, the UK, the Netherlands and Italy.

Several of the world's major cattle countries are ranching nations, farming beef cattle on a grand scale. In many of these, British breeds have been hugely influential: beef cows like the HEREFORD, ANGUS and SHORTHORN were exported all over the world in great numbers from the 18th century onwards and thrived even in subtropical climates.

In North America waves of settlers brought their own cows, and British cattle accompanied the Pilgrim Fathers in the 1620s. British breeds were soon pouring across the Atlantic into North America, and quickly spread from the east coast right across the continent.

Above: Ranchers driving a cattle herd in the Big Belt Mountains, Montana, USA.

Although Australia initially imported a handful of Indian ZEBU, by 1900 the country's 8.6 million cattle were almost all of traditional British breeds. More Indian ZEBU were imported in the 1950s and soon became of major importance in the northern areas when crossed with the British breeds.

Those who are used to the appearance of European cattle are surprised when they come across Asian and African breeds with humps. Wild aurochs bulls had no more of a hump than any European bull's 'crest' today, but in hotter climates a combination of farmers' preference and environmental influence encouraged fatty humps to develop in both bulls and cows. It started to the east of Mesopotamia, then spread into India, where local ZEBU today are typical of humped cattle, and also moved via the eastern Mediterranean into Africa. In southern Africa there is also a type known as the sanga, with a smaller, muscular hump. Sanga-type humps are often seen in the crosses between zebu and the non-humped (taurine) breeds that are now common in the US and Australia.

MIXING THE BREEDS

BREEDERS ARE NEVER SATISFIED. ALTHOUGH MANY traditional breeds have proved themselves over the past two centuries, they have had to adapt to changing markets – British breeds like the ABERDEEN-ANGUS and HEREFORD were almost stunted in the mid-20th century to suit mainly the market in Argentina. But in North America they were deemed too squat and were bred much taller.

In the US there has been experimentation in creating new breeds for local conditions by combining existing ones – either mixtures of European breeds, or more radically by crossing these with humped zebu. The first all-American new beef breed was the BRAHMAN, created from a mixture of ZEBU originating in India and Pakistan with assorted European breeds to improve the heat tolerance of the latter.

A recent US trend has been to turn existing breeds black instead of, say, their characteristic red or yellow, and to infuse the polled gene into countless breeds. This is mostly achieved by crossbreeding with that old favourite from Scotland, the ABERDEEN-ANGUS.

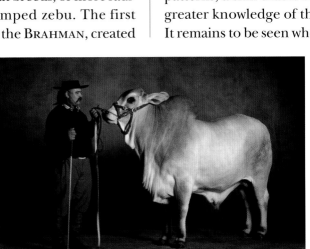

Above: The American Brahman has been widely used to create new breeds in the USA, Latin America and Australia.

The latest American trend is, ironically, back to smaller or 'lowline' cattle, better suited to small farms and often very like the 'stunted' British beef breeds of the 1950s the Americans were so determined to grow larger. Sometimes the trend is taken to an extreme and newcomers are described as miniatures and marketed as adorable pets. One American farm is not only creating endless new miniature 'breeds' but also patenting a phalanx of new names for those with eye-catching coat patterns. There is considerable potential in breeding for patterns, a skill that is becoming easier to acquire with greater knowledge of the genetics of coat inheritance. It remains to be seen whether these miniature cattle will maintain all their useful traits.

In Africa, there has already been plenty of infusion of both European and American breeds to 'improve' native cows, as well as efforts to turn some of the African breeds into beef animals productive enough to catch the eye of American and Australian ranchers. In the US, breeding programmes have introduced African blood into American cattle, making the national herd truly international.

A NEW WORLD

THE WORLD OF ARICULTURE HAS BECOME increasingly scientific over the past two centuries, perhaps nowhere more so than in breeding.

A problem faced by cattle breeders is that cows have a much longer gestation period (nine months) than other farm animals and usually produce a single calf. So it takes quite a while to improve or create a breed.

By the 1940s a few artificial insemination (AI) stations for dairy cattle had been set up in England and other countries. Once techniques for storing semen at very low temperatures had been perfected, AI became a powerful tool for spreading genetic merit, with each ejaculation able to provide a thousand inseminations. The large AI organisations had power over which sires should be used and they did not always pay close attention to conformation and type. Precisely because one bull could now father thousands of calves quickly, his defects could become widespread in the world's cattle population long before anybody realised what was happening. Another problem was the major loss of genetic diversity caused by the use of so few top bulls.

Then came embryo transfer: embryos from a particular mating were removed from the cow soon after conception and placed in surrogate cows. If super-ovulation was induced, the conceiving cow produced far more embryos and thus many more offspring without actually having to carry the foetuses herself.

Next came cloning, famously in 1997 with Dolly the Sheep. Since then, dairy cows have also been cloned, by removing an egg's DNA and replacing it with the DNA of an adult cell. A cow originally cloned from ear cells produced embryos that were transferred to recipient surrogate cows in the UK, resulting in the birth of eight calves during 2007 and 2008. 'Clone farming' had arrived in Britain.

What does the future hold? In April 2009 it was announced that the bovine genome had been sequenced. Scientists were excited – not only because it would have a huge impact on cow breeding, but also because the bovine genome turned out to be far closer to the human genome than that of rodents, so there was potential for using cows to 'inform research' into human health and disease.

Above: Gloria, born at an agrarian research farm outside Brasilia in 2004, was the first offspring of a cloned cow in Latin America.

SHOWS: THE EARLY YEARS

THERE HAVE ALWAYS BEEN LIVESTOCK MARKETS. In days gone by, huge numbers of cattle followed the ancient droveways, herded on foot or by horseback from remote parts of the country to wherever a good price might be obtained for them. Market towns would hold weekly livestock markets. Then came annual fairs, with livestock pouring into the area for a few days. Farmers could now take a look at everybody else's animals and see how someone had developed a certain type.

The creation of the railway network in the 19th century meant that cattle no longer had to be driven to market on foot, losing weight and condition along the way. You could load them into a wagon and send them off, either to market or to the new agricultural shows where the latest machinery and best cattle in the land were shown.

For centuries, there had been a Smithfield livestock market in fields on what was then the outskirts of London. In 1798 the Smithfield Cattle & Sheep Society was formed, at a time when the 'shearings' at Holkham and Woburn led the way as venues for farmers

Above: The grand exhibition of cattle at the Royal Agricultural Society of England, which took place in Bristol on July 14th, 1842.

to find out about breeding and feeding their livestock. Smithfield was by far the largest British fatstock market. The new society had its first Christmas show in December 1799 and some huge bullocks were exhibited: one was 6 ft 7 in tall and 8 ft 11 in long and weighed about 21 cwt; another, a HEREFORD, was 7 ft tall. Smithfield was all about meat. In 1949 the winter Smithfield Show would move to Earls Court and in 2009 to Stoneleigh.

The late 18th century had already seen the formation of a rash of local, county and regional agricultural societies, such as the Bath and West of England Society (1777), the Highland & Agricultural Society of Scotland (1783) and the Cornwall Agricultural Association (1793). In many cases the societies turned their annual meetings into livestock shows, but it was in the 19th century that agricultural shows really got going. The first Highland Show was in 1822; the first Cornwall event in 1827; and like virtually all the big shows that followed them, they were peripatetic, held at different venues in their region each year. Most shows did not find permanent grounds until the 1950s and '60s.

SUMMER SHOWS

IN 1838 THE ENGLISH AGRICULTURAL SOCIETY (later the Royal Agricultural Society of England) was founded. It began to hold annual summer Country Meetings in various parts of the country, setting up a pattern of itinerant Royal Shows in rotation in both metropolitan and rural areas, before settling down with its own permanent showground at Stoneleigh in 1963.

Other major summer shows established in the same era included the Stithians Show in Cornwall (1834), Royal Norfolk Show (1847), and Newport Show (1890). More followed in the next century: the Royal Welsh (1904) and the Kent County (1929). More recently, in 1970 the East of England Show merged several 19th-century agricultural societies. The shows grew, not just in terms of the space needed for the crowds that came through their gates, but also in duration: a few grew from one-day meetings to two, three or even four days – plenty of time to create a sense of camaraderie among exhibitors. Livestock remain at the heart of the summer shows, which also have exhibits of farm machinery and cover the full gamut of agricultural interests. Livestock judging is still the main feature but there are other events to entertain visitors, some not directly or even remotely relevant to farming.

In Australia the emphasis is more agricultural and cow-oriented, with a whole range of Royal shows in state capitals, some lasting for two weeks. New Zealand has its own Royal Show and the Auckland Royal Easter Show.

Perhaps the most cow-oriented of all are the American shows, where most of the big events usually include rodeos and are not summer affairs. The six-day American Royal is held in Kansas City, Missouri, in October. In November there is the two-week North American International Livestock Exposition at Louisville, Kentucky. The National Western Stock Show is held in Denver, Colorado, over most of the month of January. Three-week Texan livestock shows include the long-established Southwestern Exposition at Fort Worth in January/February. And one of the world's major livestock events is in France: the Paris International Agricultural Show, which was first held in 1870, takes place at the end of February.

Above: The summer South of England Show has taken place at Ardingly, Sussex, since 1967: it attracts 90,000 visitors a year.

PREPARING FOR SHOWS

THE SUMMER SEASON IS THE PEAK OF ACTIVITY for many who show their cows. All the preening and pampering in the world cannot turn a poor cow into a prize-winner: she must have good breeding. Shows are where breeders catch the eye of people wanting to buy their animals, or their genetic material.

A young animal destined for the show-ring needs to be handled and halter trained from an early age. Good handling is a matter of psychology, empathy, patience and the ability to read the animal's body language and anticipate its reactions to different circumstances.

Halter training – teaching the heifer to walk with you willingly – needs to be practised frequently in small doses. She should know how to walk slowly and gracefully in the ring, with head held well up and looking alert, and how to pose for the judge with feet properly placed.

Also key is getting the heifer used to being loaded into a trailer and to seeing a handler dressed in a white coat. The aim is to ensure the animal is not under stress on the big day. A bigger problem is accustoming show-cows to a new world full of strangers,

Above: Regular grooming is part of getting a heifer used to being handled, and it also helps to build up a good hair coat.

noise, loudspeakers, strange quarters and regimes, and the extraordinary buzz and energy of the showground.

The actual preparations for making the cow look her best for the big day are based on getting her into good physical condition, with appropriate feeding so that she looks 'fit, not fat', and her coat in the very best of health even before all the grooming and shampooing.

Coat preparation in the weeks running up to the show includes frequent rinsing with water followed by brushing and combing while damp to train the hair; occasional thorough washing to get dirt out; daily brushing; and clipping to trim the coat, with 'blocking' to emphasise the cow's good points. Tail tassel tangles can be reduced by using hair conditioner after washing.

With dairy cows, there is the state of their udders to consider. The cow won't look her best in the ring with an udder bursting with milk or totally flabby: she should be milked a few hours before her ring appearance.

At the showground the allocated pen needs to be a showcase, with well-designed information boards and someone helpful on hand.

WHAT THE JUDGES LOOK FOR

THE CULMINATION OF SO MUCH PREPARATION IS the few minutes in the ring. This is where it all comes together: perfect conformation, good breeding, the right choice of animal for the show and class, knowing and obeying the rules, presenting a cow in top condition and beautifully groomed that knows how to behave, walk and pose. It is not only the cow who will be judged: it is also her handler, who needs to look as smart (if not as beautiful) as the cow.

The judge is looking for qualities that will make the animal profitable. In a dairy cow, these are a dairy-like conformation to support functional traits, i.e. good milk yields and a long and productive life. A dairy cow scorecard might be: frame (skeletal) 15 per cent, dairy character 20 per cent, body capacity (barrel and chest) 10 per cent, feet (at correct angle) and legs (properly set) 15 per cent, udder 40 per cent. In the latter, the judge is looking for depth, good 'attachment', teat shape and placement (squarely under each quarter of the udder), a level udder 'floor', balanced quarters, and a soft, pliable udder texture after milking.

Above: Beef animals should stand squarely on balanced hoofs, walk with no waddling and not have post legs, cow hocks, sickle hocks or bow legs.

The judge will take into account any characteristics that are important for a particular breed. For example, AYRSHIRE cows are known for their strongly attached, evenly balanced, flat-based udders; HOLSTEINS for their large size and clearly defined coat markings; GUERNSEYS for refinement; BROWN SWISS for being strong and vigorous; and JERSEYS for 'sharpness with strength'.

With a beef animal the emphasis is naturally on the muscling and the judge will check the head is carried well, the body is long (for more meat) and the legs are sturdy enough to carry the extra weight compared with a dairy cow. The hoof prints should be even, with the back hoof stepping into the print made by the front hoof as the cow walks. The cow should have a good jaw (indicative of sound teeth), no structural weaknesses in the joints and spine, a reasonably straight top line, rounded rump and consistent musculature the full length of the body, especially in the 'prime cut' areas, an appropriate degree of fatness (judged by the brisket, flank and tailhead) and a sensible udder. Judges are looking for depth beneath the beauty.

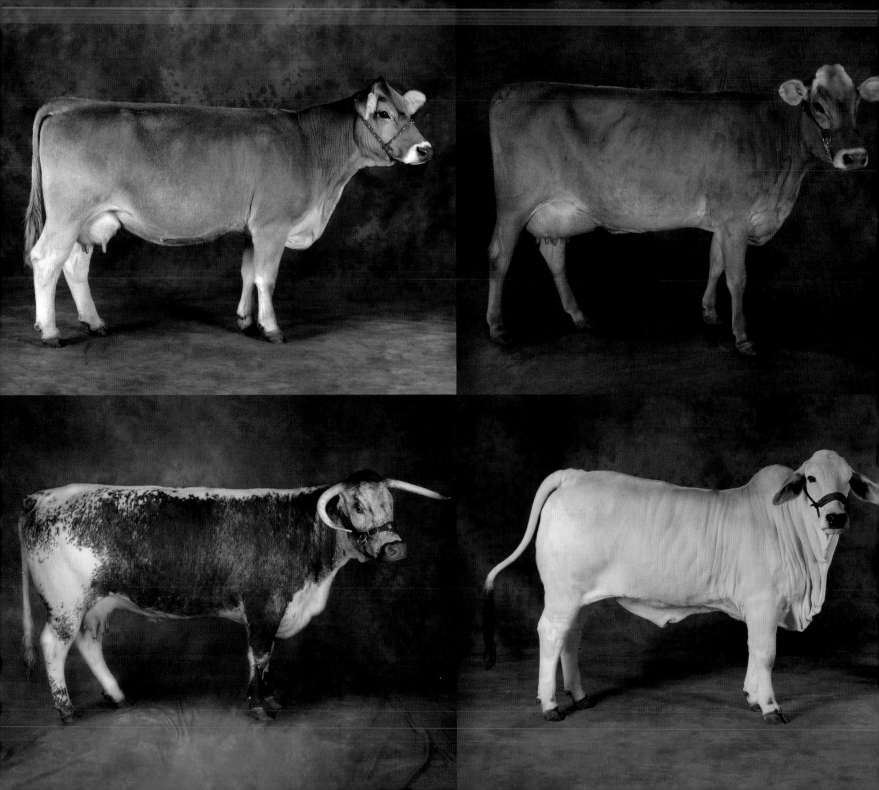

THE COWS

With their GEISHA-LIKE gait and the dreamy gaze of a *bevy of pre-Raphaelite* beauties, these *exquisite beasts* are the UNDISPUTED stars of a thousand country fairs. Far from the ORDURE of the farmyard, we can lift the curtain to reveal...

BEAUTIFUL COWS!

ANKOLE WATUSI
8-YEAR-OLD COW

Many native African cows have been selectively bred for centuries, with different tribes selecting for looks above all, such as striking coat patterns and colours. The Ankole sanga cattle of East Africa have always been bred for dramatic horns and for their milk. The most dramatic of all Ankole cattle are the WATUSI of the Tutsi tribes, now seen in Europe and the US.

Features

Watusi horns are very thick at the base. Each can be as long as 150 cm (5 ft) and the spread between their tips can be as much as 180 cm (70 in). Watusi cows usually have solid dark red coats, with occasional splashes of white, but can also be black, brown, yellow or white. They have a small hump, large ears and a long tail.

Use

In their homelands, Ankole cows are still bred mainly to produce high butterfat milk. Overseas they have been largely ornamental: they were first exported to German zoos in the 1920s, and from Europe to the US in the 1960s, where they were dubbed Ankole-Watusi. They have struck a chord in American hearts, and American breed associations are expanding their use on beef ranches.

Related Breeds

Local Ankole varieties include Bahima, Bashi and Kigezi sangas in Uganda and Zaire, and the Inkuku and sacred Inyambo Watusi cattle of Rwanda. In the US there has been some experimental crossing of Ankole-Watusi with Texas Longhorn.

Size

Bull weight .... 450–725 kg (1000–1600 lb)

Cow weight .... 410–550 kg (900–1200 lb)

Origin & Distribution

Originating around the great central lakes, especially in Uganda, Rwanda and Burundi, Ankole cattle have been exported to a few

Uganda, Rwanda, Burundi

BRAUNVIEH
4-YEAR-OLD COW

Mentioned in Swiss medieval records, BRAUNVIEH grazed higher Alpine pastures. European and North American interest led 19th-century Swiss breeders to take them more seriously, specifying that they should be brown, and supply ample milk and meat. Braunviehs were developed into the American Brown Swiss dairy cow in the US. In Switzerland they stayed dual-purpose but the spread of the Brown Swiss was relentless.

Features

Braunvieh cows are a mousy grey-brown, ranging from light to very dark. There is a pale halo around the muzzle and the underparts and poll are paler too. The horns are short and rather upright. With their muscular legs, they are sturdier than the American Brown Swiss.

Use

The 'original' Braunvieh, with no American blood, is now more a beef than dual-purpose breed in North America but remains a useful suckler cow. In Australia, Braunviehs are used to improve musculature and maternal traits in European black and grey breeds in the south and are crossed with Brahman in the north.

Related Breeds

There are local versions of the Braunvieh in many countries and it has also contributed to countless breeds worldwide, including mixtures such as the Schwyz-Zeboid (Swiss Zebu) in Tajikistan and the Braunbrah (Braunvieh and Brahman) in Australia.

Size

Bull weight .... 950–1250 kg (2100–2750 lb)

Cow weight .... 550–750 kg (1200–1650 lb)

Origin & Distribution

The traditional Braunvieh spread from eastern Switzerland into every continent: there are now more than seven million cattle of Braunvieh origin (including Brown Swiss) in 60 countries.

Switzerland

HIGHLAND

4-YEAR-OLD HEIFER

Scotland's HIGHLAND cattle are tough enough to withstand their rigorous native conditions and so hairy that they could be mistaken for yaks with horns. One of Britain's purest breeds, they have been improved by selection rather than cross-breeding. They used to be swum across the straits between islands and the mainland before the 20th century. Highland herds are called 'folds'.

Features

Many Highlands are tawny but coat colours range from cream to black. The insulating undercoat is fine and woolly and there is a wavy, shaggy, long-haired waterproof outer coat, which also covers the Highland's broad short face with a heavy sporran-like fringe. The bull's strong horns grow outwards horizontally, while the cow's are longer and finer and sweep outwards, forwards and upwards

Use

The hardy and long-lived Highland can thrive in cold and wet climates on coarse vegetation and sparse grazing where other breeds would give up. The Highland's main use is as a suckler cow to produce pure or crossbred beef calves but the cattle are also a tourist attraction in farm parks.

Related Breeds

There is a 'Miniature' Highland (under 107 cm/42 in tall) in the US. In western Scotland the Highland has been crossed with the Beef Shorthorn to create the Luing beef breed. It has also, light-heartedly, been crossed with yak to create the Yakmac.

Size

Bull weight .... 770–900 kg (1700–2000 lb)

Cow weight .... 450–590 kg (1000–1300 lb)

Origin & Distribution

The breed originated in the Scottish Highlands and islands. It has spread to the US, Australia, New Zealand, the Faroe Islands, South America and parts of Europe.

Scotland

GLOUCESTER

8-YEAR-OLD COW

Single and Double Gloucester cheeses made this old breed famous. It was one of England's better dairy cows in the 18th century but is now a rare breed. In 1796 a GLOUCESTER cow, Blossom, infected a milk-maid with cowpox and Edward Jenner, a local doctor, successfully used pus from the girl's pox blisters as the world's first smallpox vaccine. Blossom's hide is still displayed at St George's teaching hospital in Tooting.

Features

The Gloucester has a smart, short-haired mahogany coat with a white line running along the back and underside, and a white tail. Its slender dark-tipped white horns are middle-length, growing out and upwards. Its tongue and teats are black and the muzzle is slate-coloured. The forehead is broad and the nose Roman.

Use

The Gloucester has always been a good milking cow, especially for cheese production, but it is not an extreme dairy type and is now considered to be dual-purpose. Steers are sometimes trained as draught oxen on farm parks and for period films.

Related Breeds

Gloucesters are broadly similar to the extinct Glamorgan cows of Wales. Grouped by blood type with the middle-horned red cattle of southern England, they share the white finchback with Hereford and old English Longhorn cattle.

Size

Bull weight .... 750 kg (1655 lb)

Cow weight .... 500 kg (1100 lb)

Origin & Distribution

The western English county of Gloucestershire is this cow's ancestral home and it has not strayed far from it except to other British counties.

Gloucestershire, England

DEVON

6-YEAR-OLD COW

The classic red breed of southern England, DEVON cattle set sail from their Plymouth home port for America in 1623. In the new colony they supplied milk, meat and muscle power and were the oxen of choice on the Oregon Trail. In 1800 Devons went to South Africa and by the 1860s the breed had found its way to Mexico and Jamaica. In New Zealand, Devon oxen were used by pioneers to haul heavy timber during forest clearance.

Features

The colour of the Devon's coat is light red or chestnut to deep rich red, preferably bright 'ruby' red, with a creamy white tail switch. The muzzle is yellowish. Horns are of middle length but a polled variety has been developed.

Use

Devons are mainly used as suckler cows or as terminal sires for beef calves. As good low-input beef cows, capable of rearing their calves on grass alone, Devons are now also a popular choice for environmental and conservation grazing schemes on marginal land and unimproved pasture.

Related Breeds

Devon breeding has found its way into the Jamaica Red, the Hawaiian Makaweli and the Brazilian Santa Gabriela. It has contributed to the improvement of Japanese breeds and has had a reciprocal influence on the Salers of France.

Size

Bull weight .... 770–1000 kg (1700–2200 lb)

Cow weight .... 430–590 kg (950–1300 lb)

Origin & Distribution

Originating in southwest England, the Devon has been exported to more than 30 countries, including the US, Australia, New Zealand, Brazil, South Africa, Zimbabwe, Kenya and Jamaica.

Devon, England

SOUTH DEVON

2-YEAR-OLD HEIFER

Devon's famous clotted cream used to rely on the 'Big Red' or 'Hammer' SOUTH DEVON cows of the South Hams, a region of this English county. These large cattle were also work animals in the old days and the steers were fattened specifically to feed the industrial communities of Wales and the Midlands. They have thrived, notably in South Africa, for more than a century.

Features

Britain's largest native breed and fondly known by some as the Gentle Giant or the Orange Elephant, the docile, motherly South Devon – golden sandy to medium red – is often mistaken visually for the unrelated yellow Gelbvieh. The muzzle is pink and the short horns are cream-coloured. The fine coat occasionally shades to paler areas on the underside and legs as well as around the eyes.

Use

Although South Devons were originally triple-purpose and in the first part of the 20th century used as dairy cows, breeding efforts from the 1970s concentrated on beef. There is probably only one milking herd left in England; otherwise it is a beef breed, used purebred or crossed as suckler cows.

Related Breeds

The Hammer is related to the 'Ruby Red' Devon and has links with Channel Island breeds, especially Guernsey. It is now crossed with everything from British and Continental breeds to Afrikander and Brahman (for example, the South Bravon).

Size

Bull weight .... 1200–1600 kg (2600–3500 lb)

Cow weight .... 635–725 kg (1400–1600 lb)

Origin & Distribution

South Devons originated in southwest England and are now found on five continents, with breed societies in Canada, the US, South Africa, Australia, New Zealand and South America.

Devon, England

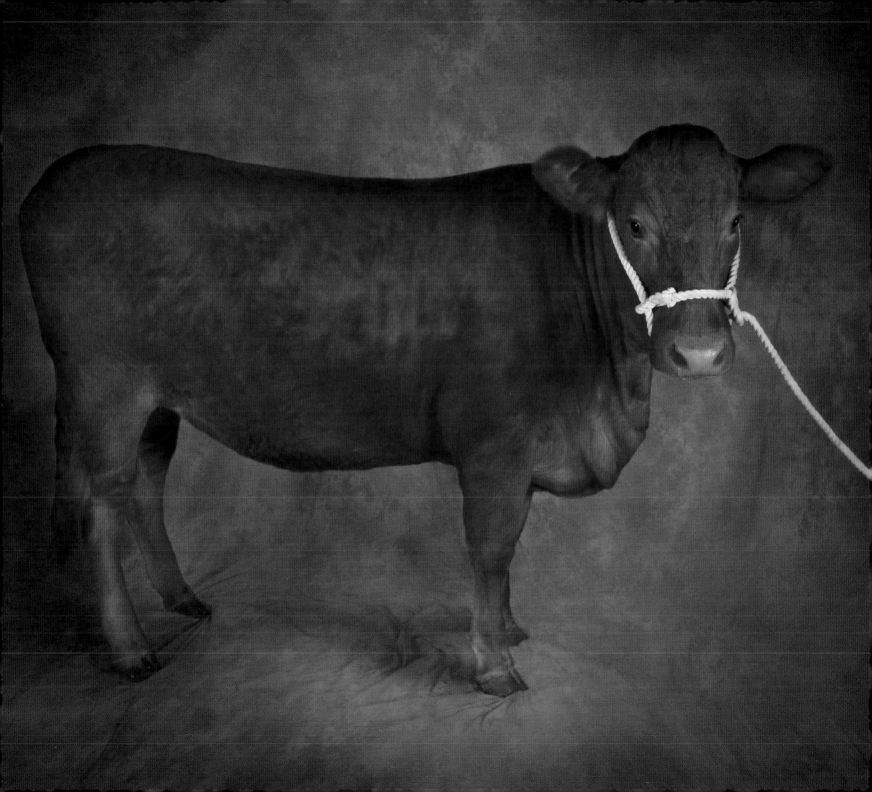

SUSSEX

2-YEAR-OLD HEIFER

An old middle-horned red breed from the south of England, the Sussex developed into a bigger breed to suit the heavy Wealden clays, especially when dragging the plough: it had powerful shoulder muscles and very strong legs. These oxen were invaluable to the medieval local iron industry for hauling weighty loads of metal and timber, yet in the early 19th century a Sussex ox ran four miles in 16 minutes on the Lewes racecourse.

Features

Not unlike the Devon but bigger and not quite so 'tidy', Sussex cows have very deep red/brown coats with smart white tail switches. The fine summer coat grows thick and curly in winter and the cows also thrive in hot climates.

Use

Hardy, self-reliant Sussex cows are popular for use in extensive and organic systems, rearing their own calves and helping with conservation grazing on scrubby or marshy land. They are also popular overseas, especially in the northwestern province of South Africa, where Sussex cattle turn grass into beef.

Related Breeds

Sussex cows have particularly close links with the 'Ruby Reds' of north Devon. The Sabre of Texas is a cross between the Sussex and Brahman. There is a Polled Sussex variety, created by crossing with Aberdeen-Angus.

Size

Bull weight .... (average) 950 kg (2090 lb)

Cow weight .... (average) 585 kg (1290 lb)

Origin & Distribution

From their home county in southern England, Sussex cows have spread in limited numbers to North and South America, Australia, New Zealand and eastern and (especially) southern Africa.

Sussex, England

SALERS

5-YEAR-OLD COW

The Salers is notably different to most other French breeds and has a long history. It began as a tough mountain breed isolated in the Massif Central, where the herds were moved ceremoniously to higher grazing in the summer with much festivity: the horns of Salers cows would be beribboned and their cowbells mingled with village band music as they wandered through the streets.

Features

Two major features of these good-looking cows are their curving horns and their curly deep mahogany coats (in North America both have been altered and many are now polled, black and smooth-haired)! The pelvis is unusually wide, so the cows calve easily.

Use

In the mountains these were originally all-purpose cows but the Salers, always quite large for a mountain type, is now mainly a beef breed, though in some places it is a dairy cow. The breed has only recently been used in other countries but is rapidly increasing, especially in North America for beef. Salers cows cope well with climate extremes, both cold and hot.

Related Breeds

The Salorn, recognised as a new breed in 1986, is based on three-eighths Texas Longhorn and five-eighths Salers. The Salerford is simply a crossbreed resulting from using a Salers bull on a Hereford cow.

Size

Bull weight .... 1000–1200 kg (2200–2600 lb)

Cow weight .... 650–850 kg (1430–1870 lb)

Origin & Distribution

From France's Auvergne region the Salers has spread to North America, Australia, New Zealand, southern Africa, Ireland, the UK and other European countries.

Auvergne, France

LIMOUSIN

4-YEAR-OLD COW

Strictly speaking, the name of this French breed should be pronounced 'Limooza'. The name refers to the west central region of France, near the city of Limoges. LIMOUSIN cows are typical of central France, where most cattle were solid-coloured horned draught animals on smallholdings. A Limousin bull attracted a price of 50,000 guineas in 2008.

Features

Limousin cows have a sandy look to them: their coats are 'wheat-red' – mostly dark golden red but with lighter 'wheat' colouring around the eyes, the pink muzzle and the underparts. The horns are of medium length, growing outwards and then turning forwards. There is also a popular Black Limousin (often with brown hairs) in North America, where most Limousins are polled.

Use

In earlier times Limousin oxen were noted for being fast as well as strong, but the emphasis has been on beef since the end of the 19th century and they are now one of France's two major beef breeds. Limousin cows are widely used in suckler herds and the bulls currently dominate the beef herd in the UK and other countries. Limousin suckler cows are said to age gracefully.

Related Breeds

There are possible links between Limousins and the Blonde d'Aquitaine and yellow breeds of Austria and Germany. The Brahmousin and Bravado originated from crosses of Brahman zebu and Limousin, and the 'Lim-Flex' is a Limousin/Angus hybrid.

Size

Bull weight .... 860–1100 kg (1900–2400 lb)

Cow weight .... 500–590 kg (1100–1300 lb)

Origin & Distribution

From central France, Limousins have spread to Australia, New Zealand, North and South America, South Africa, Zimbabwe, Russia, the UK and many other European countries.

central France

CHAROLAIS
2-YEAR-OLD HEIFER

France's heavy white CHAROLAIS led the Continental charge into the world's beef herds in the late 1950s. Selectively bred by farmers around Charolle in the 18th century, these hefty cattle crossed the Atlantic in 1930, imported into Mexico by Frenchman Jean Pugibet, who had served in the Great War. The celebrated King Ranch and other Texans imported some of his white bulls in 1936.

Features

Colour and size are the eye-catching characteristics of Charolais cows. These massive animals have large frames and long bodies; their coat is white to cream or pale straw and the muzzle is pink. The horns are short to medium in length. The large-eyed cows look decidedly maternal, but they have never excelled as milk producers.

Use

The major role of the Charolais worldwide is as a terminal sire: the bulls are mated with cows of other (usually traditional British) breeds to produce fast-growing muscular beef calves. The bulls 'colour mark' their offspring: they dilute calves from red cows to a salmony or pale coffee colour and those from black ones to creamy soot, but keeping the mother's coat pattern.

Related Breeds

Exotic new breeds created with Charolais blood include the Charbray, Charford, CharSwiss, Charollandais and Brazil's Canchim, and there are bits of Charolais in several other American, Canadian, Australian and Ukrainian breeds – and even in experimental crosses with wild banteng and American buffalo.

Size

Bull weight .... 900–1200 kg (2000–2650 lb)

Cow weight .... 570–900 kg (1250–2000 lb)

Origin & Distribution

The Charolais originated in central France around Charolle, and has spread to North and Latin America, most of Europe, the former USSR, Australia, New Zealand, Japan and southern Africa.

central France

SIMMENTAL
3-YEAR-OLD COW

Switzerland is the home of this gentle but rugged cow: the all-purpose SIMMENTALS originated in the Simme Valley and before the 19th century were generally known as Bernese. There are now more than 40 million of them worldwide. A Simmental cow born in Switzerland in 1915 produced at the age of 14 a phenomenal 11,902 kg (26,000 lbs) of milk in what was to be her last lactation – she kept on pouring it out for 498 days.

Features

The most obvious mark of a Simmental is the white face, which bulls pass on to all their offspring. Coat colours range from yellow-leather to dun-red, always marked with white, including legs and tail. American Simmentals are mainly black or dark red.

Use

Simmentals used to be all-purpose but then became dual-purpose for beef and dairy in Europe. In most of Europe, Simmental cows are still milky, but British and American Simmentals have been developed as a beef breed and terminal sire. In Australia the cow is used in crossbreeding to improve cows' milking qualities.

Related Breeds

The Simmental was the ancestor of France's Montbéliard and Germany's Fleckvieh cows. It has been widely used in crossbreeding to create new breeds and has influenced many others, especially national breeds called 'Red Pied' in local languages.

Size

Bull weight ... 1000–1400 kg (2200–3000 lb)

Cow weight ... 500–860 kg (1100–1900 lb)

Origin & Distribution

The Simmental originated in Berne, Switzerland, and has spread worldwide to North and South America, Australia, New Zealand, China, southern Africa, the Middle East and most of Europe.

Berne, Switzerland

TEXAS LONGHORN
4-YEAR-OLD COW

Think cowboy, and you think TEXAS LONGHORN: they are forever associated with the romance of the Wild West but their history dates back to Spanish cattle brought over by explorers in sailing ships to Santo Domingo in the 1490s and later into Mexico. In about 1690, herds of these 'criollo' cattle were driven from Mexico to the Sabine River and what would become Texas.

Features

The most obvious badge of a Texas Longhorn is the long handlebar horns, spreading outwards and upwards with at least 100 cm (40 inches) between the tips. The cows have long legs for range-walking and a free-and-easy gait. There are all sorts of 'wild flamboyant' colours and patterns in the short straight slick coat; the most common is red with assorted white patches and speckles.

Use

Longhorns are most often seen in rodeos, on film sets and in conservation herds, but they are winning their way back on to ranches, recognised for their naturally lean meat, easy calving, longevity and survival instincts. Increasingly they are seen as a source of genetic material for the future of the beef industry.

Related Breeds

There is no relationship between the Texas Longhorn and the Longhorn of Britain but links exist with the Florida Cracker, an old Spanish criollo. New synthetics include the Texon (with Devon), the Salorn (with Salers) and the Geltex (with Gelbvieh).

Size

Bull weight ... 590–1100 kg (1300–2500 lb)

Cow weight ... 320–725 kg (700–1600 lb)

Origin & Distribution

Texas Longhorns originated from old Spanish herds that drifted into Texas. Imported into Canada and Australia in the 19th century, they are only seen scattered in zoos and farm parks elsewhere.

Texas, USA

JERSEY

2-YEAR-OLD HEIFER

The island of Jersey, a British dependency just off the French coast, is known worldwide for its distinctive cows: there are, for example, 600,000 JERSEY cows in New Zealand and 400,000 in the US. There is a theory that, since fishermen from Jersey were fishing off Newfoundland in the 15th century, perhaps Jersey cows landed in Canada much earlier than officially recorded.

Features

Jersey cows are very dainty and as bony as catwalk models, with slender legs, 'deer-like' heads, dished faces and doe-like eyes. Coat colours are mainly fawn but range from very pale grey or silver to smoky and mulberry, occasionally broken with white. The muzzle is black, with a characteristic pale halo; the tail switch and tongue are preferably dark. Jerseys have small crumpled horns.

Use

Jerseys are dairy cows and their milk is rich in butterfat, calcium and protein; they are a favourite with cheesemakers. They yield more milk per unit of body weight than other breeds and have a long productive life. Jerseys can adapt to the hottest of climates. They may be related to Iberian, North African or Asian cows.

Related Breeds

Closely linked to the Guernsey, the Jersey has been instrumental in the formation of numerous new tropical breeds – many of them zebu crosses in the Caribbean, South America, Australia and Asia – and an influence on many others worldwide.

Size

Bull weight ... 500–815 kg (1100–1800 lb)

Cow weight ... 360–545 kg (800–1200 lb)

Origin & Distribution

Jerseys evolved on the English Channel island of Jersey and have now spread literally worldwide: it is the second most numerous dairy breed in the world after the Holstein.

Jersey

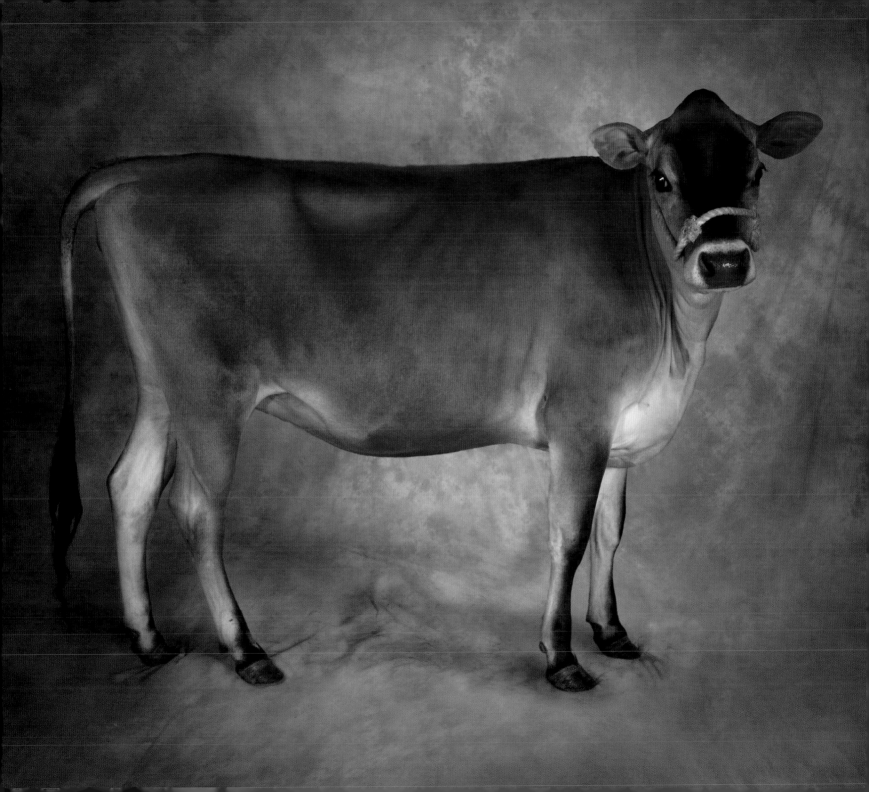

GUERNSEY

2-YEAR-OLD HEIFER

Less numerous than its Jersey neighbour but equally widespread, the 'Golden GUERNSEY' is now rapidly giving way to the ubiquitous Holstein in the dairy world. The cow's origins are probably in Normandy and Brittany. In the 17th century Guernsey cattle went to Brazil with the Baron of Nova Friburgo. They had become the major European dairy breed there by the 1950s.

Features

Golden is the Guernsey theme: golden milk and also a patched golden and white coat (the gold ranging from orange to lemon, fawn or red), amber hooves, sandy eyelashes and deep yellow skin pigmentation. Guernseys are typical dairy cows in conformation, graceful rather than pretty, with short horns. The beautiful cow shown here is three-quarters Guernsey and one-quarter Holstein; her coat colour and pattern are not typical of the pure Guernsey.

Use

Guernsey cows are pure dairy cows, and traditionally they produce milk efficiently from grazing, but they are equally productive under more intensive management. Their milk has a high beta carotene content and is rich in butterfat and protein.

Related Breeds

The Guernsey has not been widely used to create or enhance other breeds, though experimental crossing with zebu cattle in tropical regions has proved successful. The Jersey is her closest relative, along with northern French breeds.

Size

Bull weight ... 600–850 kg (1300–1800 lb)

Cow weight ... 450–600 kg (990–1100 lb)

Origin & Distribution

Originally from the Channel island of Guernsey, the breed has spread to the UK, Ireland, North America, Australia, New Zealand, Brazil, South Africa, Zimbabwe, Kenya and Uganda.

Guernsey

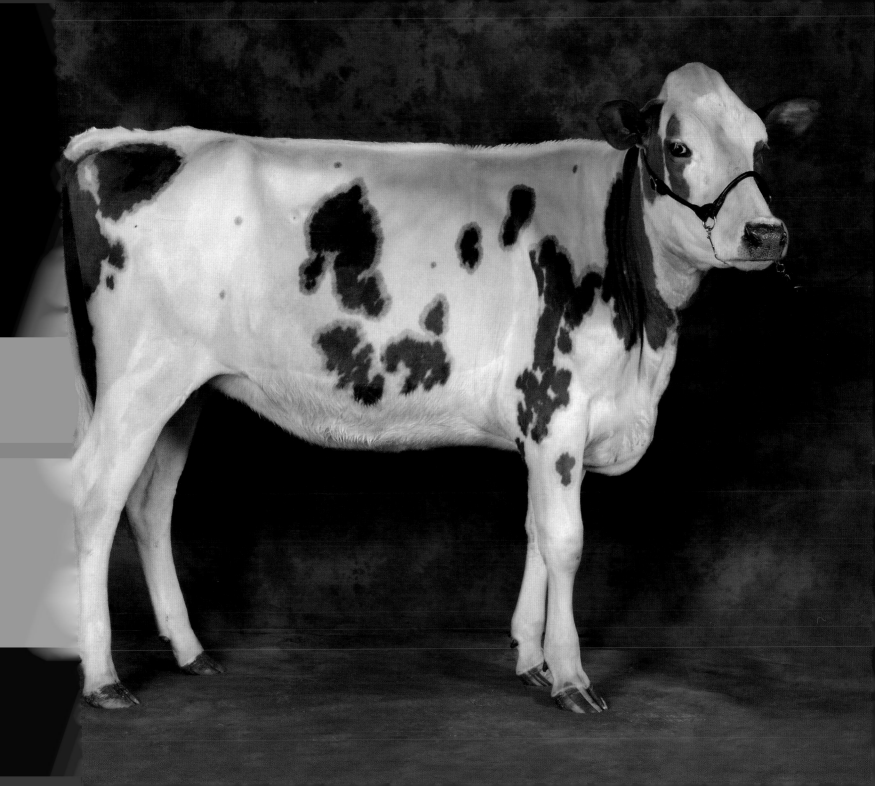

ABERDEEN-ANGUS
1-YEAR-OLD HEIFER

ABERDEEN-ANGUS cows are famous world-wide for their prime beef. This hornless black Scottish breed, which combined short-legged Buchan Humlies and hairy Angus Doddies, was exported to France, Australia and Ireland before 1820. It was introduced to the US in 1873 by capitalist George Grant when he exported four of his prize bulls to create a colony of British livestock breeders in Kansas. Many breeders returned to Scotland but their cattle remained and flourished.

Features

Aberdeen-Angus cattle are naturally polled and their coat is solid black. They vary in different parts of the world, especially in the leg length, but the conformation is blocky and muscular with a deep body. The smaller 'traditional' type is becoming rare.

Use

The pure Aberdeen-Angus is the world's prime beef breed. The bulls are also used for putting more meat on to crossbred offspring – especially in dairy herds of smaller breeds such as the Jersey, as the compact Aberdeen-Angus results in fewer calving problems.

Related Breeds

Varieties are the Red Angus and a miniature Lowline Angus. Exotic breeds include the Brangus (Angus crossed with Brahman), the Africangus (with Afrikander) and the Jamaica Black (part zebu). The Murray Grey originates from Angus and Shorthorn.

Size

Bull weight ... 820–1200 kg (1800–2650 lb)

Cow weight ... 500–700 kg (1100–1540 lb)

Origin & Distribution

The Aberdeen-Angus originated in northeast Scotland. The breed is now found worldwide but especially in the US, Argentina, Australia, New Zealand, Canada and South Africa.

northeast Scotland

AYRSHIRE
8-YEAR-OLD COW

Scotland's only native dairy breed, graceful Ayrshire cows were the darlings of the show-ring in the 19th century. The first-ever milking trial took place in Ayr in 1860: the winning cow produced 13 kg (28 lb 7 oz) of milk over five days. In 1929, two Ayrshire cows were walked from Brandon, Vermont, to the National Dairy Show at St Louis, Missouri, as a publicity stunt. Both cows went on to beat milk-yield records of their time.

Features

The Ayrshire cow's silky coat is white with clearly defined patches of red, mahogany or brown; some cows are almost all white. Her conformation is typical of dairy cows and she is fine-boned, though not as bony as Jerseys and Holsteins. The famously 'tidy' udder is long (front to back) as well as deep, level and firmly attached.

Use

Though originally of two types – a larger practical dairy cow and a smaller lightweight show-ring cow – today's Ayrshire is a commercial dairy cow with good butterfat yields. Bulls are mated with Boran zebu cows in Kenya and Sahiwal zebu cows in Pakistan.

Related Breeds

This Scottish cow is the foundation of the Finnish Ayrshire (found in large numbers in the former USSR) and the Swedish Ayrshire. It has contributed to several red or red-and-white Scandinavian breeds and to the Japanese Black.

Size

Bull weight ... 840 kg (1850 lb)

Cow weight ... 455–590 kg (1000–1300 lb)

Origin & Distribution

Ayrshires originated in southwest Scotland. They are now found in every climate from subarctic to tropical, with breed societies in North and South America, Europe, Africa and Australasia.

southwest
Scotland

BELTED GALLOWAY

8-YEAR-OLD COW

Immediately identifiable by the white belt around its middle, the BELTED GALLOWAY or 'Beltie' is a milkier version of the black Galloway. Belted cattle have been recorded in Scotland since the late 18th century and possibly acquired the coat pattern from imported Dutch Lakenvelder cattle.

Features

The soft wavy coat is usually black (also red or dun) with a full broad white belt, a pattern that makes the cattle visible in the distance in poor weather. The black is tinged with brown in summer and the coat is double, with a mossy undercoat; it is said that a Belted Galloway cow is insulated by 4,000 hairs to the square inch. Like all Galloways, the Belted is polled.

Use

Traditionally, Scottish villagers selected belted cattle as house cows and there are some commercial herds of milking Belted Galloways. More often this dual-purpose breed is farmed as suckler cows, rearing either pure or crossbred beef calves. They are hardy upland cows, well protected from cold weather and productive on rough grazing; these easy-care attributes make them a popular choice for conservation grazing schemes.

Related Breeds

Closely related to the original black Galloway, the Beltie is often crossed with Whitebred Shorthorn to produce Blue-Grey suckler cows that are in turn crossed with Continental beef sires to produce beefier calves. There is a Miniature Belted Galloway.

Size

Bull weight ... 815–955 kg (1800–2100 lb)

Cow weight ... 400–600 kg (880–1320 lb)

Origin & Distribution

Originating in southwest Scotland, the Belted variety was recognised as a separate breed in 1921. It is now found in the UK, North America, New Zealand, Australia and Switzerland.

Scotland

HEREFORD

3-YEAR-OLD COW

Τhis Welsh Marches breed stamped its famous white face on beef herds from the ranches of the American West and South American pampas to plains of Africa in the 19th century. HEREFORDS were considered 'pleasant, cheerful, open' in the 1850s, but the progeny of a Hereford bull crossed with a Kyloe cow were 'extremely pugnacious'.

Features

The Hereford's characteristic white face is passed on to any crossbred calves. Purebred cows have a rich red coat, with further areas of white on the brisket, underside, feet and tail switch and sometimes a partial white back stripe. Horns are of middle length, gently curving in the cow, and there is also a Polled Hereford. 'Traditional' Herefords (with no overseas influence) remain stocky and sturdy and now have a separate register in the UK.

Use

Originally triple-purpose, Herefords are great grazing animals and are seen in suckler herds rearing beef calves. Bulls are popular as terminal sires. A major role for them in some countries is to produce Black Baldies – a cross between Hereford heifers and a black bull, usually Angus, for beef calves.

Related Breeds

Scores of newer breeds worldwide have a dash (or much more) of Hereford. Unusual among them are Brahman and other zebu mixtures, bison crosses and Afrikander sanga combinations (Belmont Red, Bonsmara and Nuras).

Size

Bull weight ... 860–1300 kg (1900–2900 lb)

Cow weight ... 450–825 kg (990–1800 lb)

Origin & Distribution

From its English home county of Herefordshire on the Welsh borders, the breed has spread quite literally worldwide.

Herefordshire, England

LONGHORN
4-YEAR-OLD COW

Not to be confused with the Texas Longhorn, the LONGHORN is solidly English and was Britain's first true cattle breed, developed by 18th-century breeder Robert Bakewell of Leicestershire, specifically for the butcher. His most famous Longhorn bull was Twopenny, but a later, more valuable bull was Twopenny's grandson, named 'D' (which, of course, stood for penny).

Features

The dramatic horns of the Longhorn grow every which way – sweeping outwards and upwards, or curving outwards and downwards in the 'bonnet' style, or drooping like spaniels' ears, or in the chaotic 'waghorn' style with one horn growing out and up and the other out and down. The colour of the longish coat is light red roan to dark brindle, with a gleaming white finchback, a fuzzy white 'hough' spot on each thigh, and a white tail.

Use

Longhorn cows are a beef breed, with cows rearing their own calves in extensively managed suckler herds producing lean beef cheaply from grass; they are hardy and calve easily. These amiable cows are also popular as features in parkland landscapes.

Related Breeds

The Longhorn shares its roan coat with the Shorthorn, but there are no close relatives of the Longhorn in Britain, nor is it related to the Texas Longhorn. The polled Irish Moiled is remarkably similar in coat colour and pattern.

Size

Bull weight ... 1000–1100 kg (2200–2400 lb)

Cow weight ... 500–800 kg (1100–1760 lb)

Origin & Distribution

Longhorns originated in northwest and central England and spread throughout the UK and Ireland. There are isolated herds in Germany, the Benelux countries, Australia, New Zealand and the US.

northwest & central England

DAIRY SHORTHORN

5-YEAR-OLD COW

Historically the Shorthorn is probably the most famous breed of cattle in the world. Old Teeswater (famed for their milk yields) and large-buttocked Holderness cows were blended to become the Durham, later called Shorthorn. In the 18th century these were bred selectively for more milk or meat, diverging into the DAIRY SHORTHORN and Beef Shorthorn respectively.

Features

Dairy Shorthorns are down-to-earth cows, with a range of roan, red, white, red-and-white or roan-and-white coats. They have short horns, though polled varieties have been developed. In the US, the Milking Shorthorn is becoming increasingly an angular dairy type, partly due to being infused with Red Holstein genes.

Use

Dairy Shorthorns are at heart dual-purpose cows, giving plenty of milk as well as rearing beefy calves. The cows are hardy natives, good foragers, easy calvers, with a long productive life and as pretty as a picture. Recent genetic improvements have encouraged commercial dairy farmers in the UK to use more Dairy Shorthorns again, especially on organic farms.

Related Breeds

The rare Northern Dairy Shorthorn is at home on the coarse upland grazing in the Dales and is specifically for milk. In the US, the Milking Shorthorn has been officially a dairy type since 1969. Countless breeds worldwide have absorbed Shorthorn blood to improve or create them.

Size

Bull weight ... 900 kg (2000 lb)

Cow weight ... 590–635 kg (1300–1400 lb)

Origin & Distribution

All the Shorthorns (both dairy and beef) originated in northeast England and have spread worldwide.

northeast England

BEEF SHORTHORN

3-YEAR-OLD COW

When the Shorthorn breeders began to diverge in the 18th century, the Booth family in Yorkshire went for fleshiness in their cows. In the 19th century, Amos Cruickshank in Aberdeenshire followed suit; his chunkier cattle were the first 'Scotch Shorthorns' that went to North America. In many countries the breed, known as BEEF SHORTHORN in the UK since 1958, is still known as the Scotch Shorthorn or simply as the Shorthorn.

Features

A sturdier animal than the Dairy Shorthorn, this beef type may be a little shorter but the coat colours are typical of all Shorthorns – roan, red, white, red-and-white or roan-and-white. There was an infusion of Maine-Anjou in the Beef Shorthorn in the UK between 1976 and 2001 to make it bigger and better muscled.

Use

As an archetypal British beef breed, Beef Shorthorn bulls are used for siring crossbred beef calves and the cows have an important role as sucklers. In Australia, the breed has adapted well to tropical and subtropical climates, as indeed the Shorthorns have done worldwide.

Related Breeds

The rare Whitebred Shorthorn was selected within the Shorthorns of Cumberland as a white crossing sire to produce Blue-Grey cows for beef suckler herds. The Lincolnshire Red Shorthorn is now the Lincoln Red beef breed. Shorthorns in general have contributed to many, many other breeds worldwide.

Size

Bull weight .... 800 kg (1760 lb)

Cow weight .... 500 kg (1100 lb)

Origin & Distribution

From its original base in northeast England and in Scotland, the Beef Shorthorn has spread worldwide in huge numbers but is now almost rare in the UK.

northeast England & Scotland

LINCOLN RED
6-YEAR-OLD COW

The Lincoln Red was once specifically bred to produce lots of milk. In the 18th century big Old Lincolnshire pied cows were mated with red Shorthorn bulls and became the Lincolnshire Red Shorthorn. By the 1940s the breed was dual-purpose and the cows defiantly remained large when other breeds became stocky and short-legged.

Features

These large-framed cherry-red cows have broad foreheads, short faces, wide shoulders, strong necks and quite large hooves. They occasionally have short horns but most are polled, the result of deliberate crossbreeding with red or black Angus bulls in the 1930s (the word Shorthorn was dropped from the breed name in 1960).

Use

The Lincoln Red is now a beef breed (the last registered dairy type was in the 1960s) and an 'easy-care' suckler cow. The old dual-purpose type had become a beef breed by 1980 and has since been crossed with selected European breeds to improve its beef status, to such an extent that in 1998 the Rare Breeds Survival Trust began to record the 'traditional' 100 per cent native-bred type, which is on the Trust's 'Watch' list as vulnerable.

Related Breeds

The Beevbilde was a mixture of Polled Lincoln Red and Polled Beef Shorthorn. In Hungary (a country that also liked Lincolnshire pigs) the Pankota Red was based on the Lincoln Red.

Size

Bull weight .... 900 kg (1990 lb)

Cow weight .... 700 kg (1540 lb)

Origin & Distribution

The Lincoln Red originated in eastern England and has been exported to South Africa, Argentina, Uruguay, Brazil, the US, Canada, Australia, New Zealand, Germany and Hungary.

eastern England

BRITISH WHITE

7-YEAR-OLD COW

A tangled tale of abbeys, parks and stately halls created the hornless BRITISH WHITE, which had its 18th-century roots at Whalley Abbey, Lancashire, and Gunton Park, Norfolk; then, in the 19th century, at Blickling and Woodbastwick, both also in Norfolk. Classified as a rare breed in the 1970s, the British White's growing renown has upgraded it to a minority breed.

Features

A gentle colour-pointed breed, white with usually black (sometimes red) ears, eyelids, muzzle, teats and feet, British White cows often have coloured freckling over the neck, shoulders, flanks and back. The blue or dark skin and white coat help them to tolerate hot climates but they are equally hardy in cold ones. The breed is differentiated from White Park cattle by being naturally polled.

Use

Though once proudly used as a commercial milking cow, the British White has always produced beef as well. Today, the bulls are used as sires on both beef and dairy heifers and to pass the breed's polling factor and milkiness to heifers bred as suckler cows. The breed has quite high twinning rates.

Related Breeds

Often mixed with White Park herds in the past, the British White parted company in 1946 and a separate breed society was established. In the US there remains confusion between the two.

Size

Bull weight .... 815–1050 kg (1800–2300 lb)

Cow weight .... 455–680 kg (1000–1500 lb)

Origin & Distribution

Mainly originating in East Anglia and Cheshire, more anciently in Lancashire, the British White is now found in the US, Australia and Canada. It was long ago exported to Brazil, Colombia and Kenya.

East Anglia & Cheshire, England

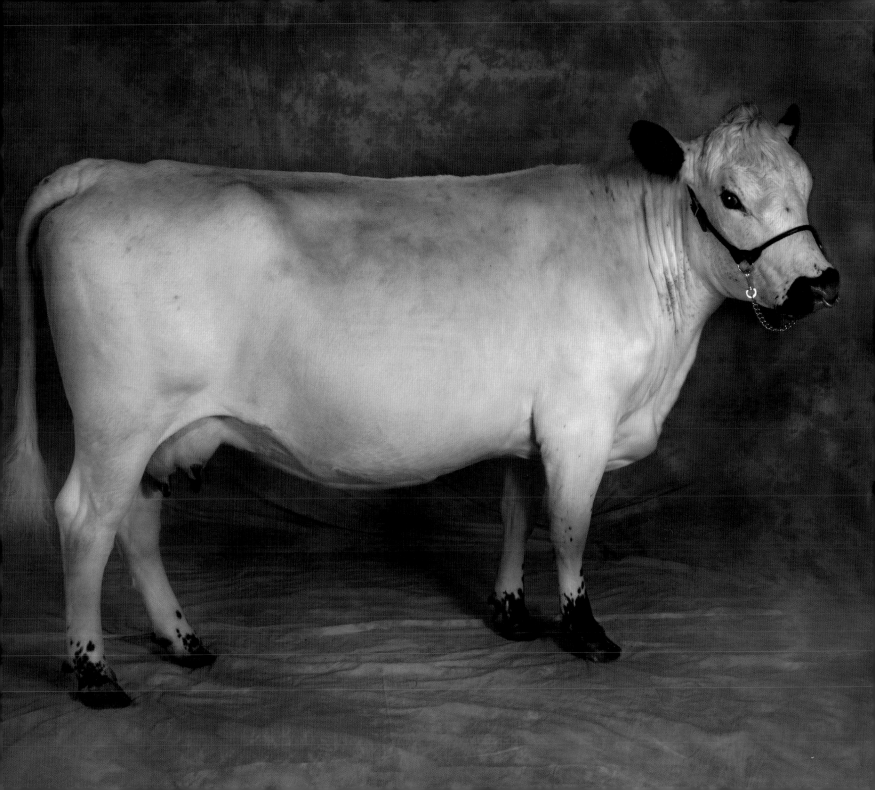

RED POLL

7-YEAR-OLD COW

RED POLLS evolved in the 19th century from a combination of two old East Anglian breeds: the milky hornless Suffolk Dun, and the blood-red beefy middle-horned Norfolk Red. The combination of being red and hornless made the Red Poll a popular rancher's choice in the American West. Latin America also gave a warm welcome to this very useful cow, using it to create new breeds.

Features

Red Polls have a dark red coat, flesh-coloured muzzle, pigmented skin, an occasional white tail switch, usually a fringe over the forehead, and strictly no horns – or even a hint of horns such as scurs. The conformation can be described as 'dairy type with extra flesh'. There was a time when Red Poll udders were notoriously baggy, possibly because they often suckled two calves at once.

Use

Traditionally the perfect dual-purpose cow, Red Polls are milky enough to join the dairy herd but also suckler cows for beef. There are still purebred milking herds in many parts of the world. Bulls can be terminal sires to encourage early calving in dairy herds or to fix red coat colour and the polled factor in other breeds.

Related Breeds

The Red Poll is an essential element in several new breeds in Latin America and the Caribbean, including Pitangueiras, Jamaica Red, La Velasquez, Senepol (created by crossing the Red Poll with the humpless long-horned N'Dama of Senegal) and Romosinuano.

Size

Bull weight .... 620–1000 kg (1300–2200 lb)

Cow weight .... 500–600 kg (1100–1300 lb)

Origin & Distribution

Originating in Norfolk and Suffolk, the Red Poll has spread to North and South America, Australia, New Zealand, southern and eastern Africa and several European countries.

Norfolk & Suffolk, England

DEXTER

4-YEAR-OLD COW

The DEXTER is immediately recognisable: if a cow is very small and black she's likely to be a Dexter. In recent years there has been a trend to smaller cows for small farmers and backyard cow keepers. The Dexter is the smallest breed in Britain and is named after Lord Hawarden's 18th-century land agent, who deliberately selected smaller animals from the ancient Kerry race of Celtic milch cows and bred them for beef and milk.

Features

Most Dexters are solid black, but solid red and dun are also acceptable colours for pedigree cows. They are middle-horned and there is a polled variety. Size is the Dexter's distinctive feature: they are only waist-high at 36–42 inches, but well proportioned.

Use

The Dexter is used for both milk and beef and sometimes as a draught animal. Some people specialise in dairy cows but most use them as sucklers whose offspring produce small joints of meat. Cows can be crossed with native beef breeds, but Continental bulls are chosen with care to avoid calving problems for small mothers.

Related Breeds

Some breeders are experimenting with colour-pointed, white and belted Dexters. 'Miniature' cows are now being bred more seriously in the US, many of them with the help of Dexter bulls.

Size

Bull weight .... 430–500 kg (950–1100 lb)

Cow weight .... 320–365 kg (700–800 lb)

Origin & Distribution

The Dexter evolved from Kerry in southwest Ireland. It is popular in the UK, US and South Africa and has spread to Australia, New Zealand, South America, Kenya, Zimbabwe and Europe.

southwest Ireland

WELSH BLACK
9-YEAR-OLD COW

There have been Celtic cattle in Wales for centuries and they were popular among graziers in the Midlands: herds would follow the old droveways into England and the cattle were seen as 'black gold'. By the late 19th century the main Welsh groups were tough little black Anglesey mountain cattle in the north and taller, rangier, milkier black Pembroke in the south. These were combined in 1873 to form the WELSH BLACK.

Features

The Welsh Black coat is thick, soft and fairly long and the colour ranges from jet black to a hint of chocolate or rust. The horns are of middle length. There are remnants of other colours excluded from the official Welsh Black, including white with black points, line-backed, bright orange-red, yellow dun, blue or mouse.

Use

Until the 1970s this was a dual-purpose breed; the cows are still milky but are now mainly in suckler herds. They are suited to upland areas, converting rough grazing into milk to feed their beef calves (purebred or crosses), but also do well in lowland systems.

Related Breeds

There are links with the Dynevor White Park and possibly the Gloucester. There is a Polled Welsh and small numbers of Belted Welsh, colour-pointed White Welsh and Red Welsh.

Size

Bull weight .... 860–1130 kg (1900–2500 lb)

Cow weight .... 500–635 kg (1100–1400 lb)

Origin & Distribution

Originating in Wales, the Welsh Black spread across Britain but has not been extensively exported. Some are found in Australia, New Zealand, Canada, the US and Germany and in small numbers in Denmark, Saudi Arabia, Jamaica and Uganda.

Wales

BRAHMAN

2-YEAR-OLD HEIFER

The BRAHMAN is a fusion of East and West in one very successful package. In 1849, the first oriental zebus were imported into the US. Years later, the British government gifted two Indian zebu bulls to a Louisiana plantation owner for teaching the British how to grow cotton and sugar. Gradually other Indian zebus arrived and from this widening gene pool a humped American subtropical beef breed grew: the Brahman of Texas.

Features

Brahman cows and bulls have a bean- to oval-shaped hump over the shoulders, the ears are large and drooping, and the dewlap falls in full loose folds under the throat. Coat colours vary, from almost white to almost black, but some are red, and occasionally white spotted. Muzzle, lips, tail switch and hooves are black.

Use

Brahmans have exceptional stamina and longevity. The cows are good and protective mothers out on the beef ranges. They can be shy but respond well to kind handling. They have a strong identity with the herd, and have been widely crossed to create new breeds.

Related Breeds

Several Indian zebu breeds contributed to the American Brahman. Numerous new breeds have resulted from Brahman crosses: Santa Gertrudis, Beefmaster, American Breed, Brangus and Drought-master. There are many Brahman/European derivatives as well.

Size

Bull weight .... 725–1000 kg (1600–2200 lb)

Cow weight .... 455–635 kg (1000–1400 lb)

Origin & Distribution

The Brahman breed originated in the US and Brazil (where it is known as the Indo-Brazilian). It has spread across the world to Australia, the Pacific, the Caribbean and the Philippines.

US, Brazil

SANTA GERTRUDIS
2-YEAR-OLD COW

Out in the Wild Horse Desert of Texas, Captain Richard King established his vast King Ranch in 1853. He bred Texas Longhorns at first, improved with Hereford and Shorthorn bulls. But in the subtropical climate, the ranch found a better improver in Brahman bulls, mating them with Durham Shorthorn cows. In 1919 an outstanding cherry-red bull named Monkey was born. He was the founding bull of the new SANTA GERTRUDIS breed, named after a local creek.

Features

There is a look of the Brahman in the big Santa Gertrudis cows: their ears are larger than European breeds and tend to droop slightly. The solid-coloured coat is Monkey's own rich deep cherry and the skin has a red pigment. This skin pigmentation also helps to protect their hooded, dark eyes from sun-induced eye cancer.

Use

The cows are good mothers in beef suckler herds and their milk has a high butterfat content. They are famous babysitters: you often see a couple minding other cows' calves while they graze.

Related Breeds

Descended from a mixture of Brahman and Shorthorn, the Santa Gertrudis has contributed to the development of the Cuprem Hybrid in Nebraska.

Size

Bull weight .... 900–1270 kg (2000–2800 lb)

Cow weight .... 630–725 kg (1390–1600 lb)

Origin & Distribution

Originating in Texas, Santa Gertrudis herds are now found in many US states and a score of other countries, including Latin America, Cuba, Canada, Australia, New Zealand, South Africa and Russia.

Texas, US

HOLSTEIN

6-YEAR-OLD COW

These striking cows have had a chequered past, with much name swapping between HOLSTEIN and Friesian. 'Holstein' was first used when cows from the German province of Schleswig-Holstein followed settlers to the New World in the 19th century. In North America, Holsteins became cattle kept purely to produce milk. They have crept back across the Atlantic: Friesians made up 86 per cent of the British dairy herd in 1982 but by 2000, Holsteins had taken over.

Features

Holstein cows have black-and-white pied coats, often more white than black, usually with black ears, white lower legs and white tail tip. There is also a red-and-white variety (Red Holstein). The horns are short, but Red breeders are developing a polled type.

Use

Holsteins are pure dairy cows, bred to produce enormous quantities of milk – the highest yields in the world. The public's reaction to the very heavy physical demands made on these short-lived milk machines has caused some breeders to rethink their breeding aims.

Related Breeds

Almost every country in the world now has its own version of black-and-white Dutch dairy cows, whether Holstein, Friesian or Holstein-Friesian.

Size

Bull weight .... (average) 1000 kg (2200 lb)

Cow weight .... (average) 680 kg (1500 lb)

Origin & Distribution

Originating in Friesland and other parts of the Netherlands, the Holstein was developed as a separate pure dairy breed in Canada and the US and is now found worldwide.

The Netherlands

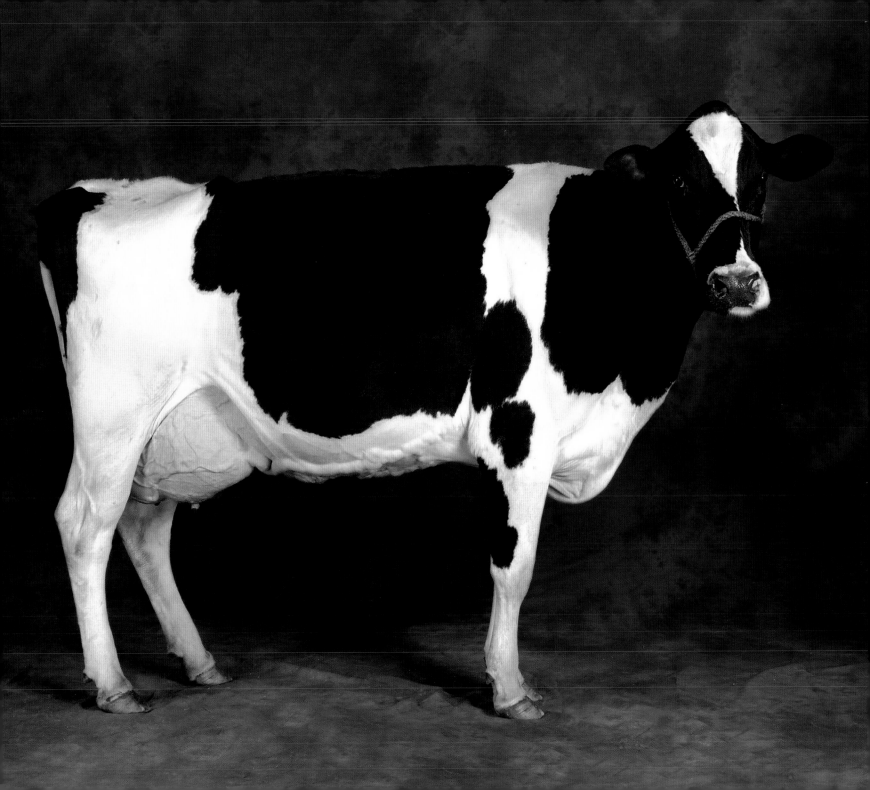

BROWN SWISS
3-YEAR-OLD COW

In the 1870s some traditional dual-purpose brown mountain cattle from the Swiss Alps were exported to North America. A US cattle breeders' association was formed in 1880 in Massachusetts, and by 1890 the type had developed into a bigger, refined dairy cow, dubbed the (American) BROWN SWISS. The ancestor of nearly all the American Brown Swiss cows today is Jane of Vernon (1929–1945), bred by Orbec Sherry of Wisconsin.

Features

The coat of Brown Swiss cows is brown to grey-brown, often with lighter colour along the back. Their pale mealy muzzle rings and dark nostrils are similar to those of Jerseys, but they are larger and much more robust-looking cows. Brown Swiss have short horns, and in the US they are taller and more dairy-like in physique than the ancestral sturdier dual-purpose cows in Europe.

Use

Bred in the US as a dairy cow and a favourite with cheesemakers, the Brown Swiss is second only to the Holstein in milk yield worldwide. The cows are known for their sound legs, feet and udders and their long productive lives.

Related Breeds

The Brown Swiss is a direct descendant of the Swiss Brown, or Braunvieh, of Switzerland and therefore related to many other national Browns.

Size

Bull weight .... 815–1130 kg (1800–2500 lb)

Cow weight .... 500–770 kg (1100–1700 lb)

Origin & Distribution

The American Brown Swiss evolved in the US. The cows are now widespread in North America and are increasingly popular in Central and South America, Europe and worldwide.

North America

GELBVIEH
1-YEAR-OLD HEIFER

GELBVIEH translates from the German as 'yellow cattle' – it was originally used as an umbrella name under which several old local varieties were combined around 1920. The family tree is complex, but broadly the Gelbvieh combined breeds from central and southern Germany, with dashes of Swiss Simmental and Swiss Brown together with several old Austrian mountain breeds and some Danish Red for good measure.

Features

Gelbvieh cows have cream to yellow to reddish gold or russet coats. The traditional honey-coloured coat is a uniform yellowish brown, with lighter areas around the eyes and muzzle, but there is also a black variety in the US and Australia. Increasingly, Gelbvieh are being bred polled with the help of the black Angus.

Use

The Gelbvieh in its homeland settled into two upland types: dual-purpose and beef. The cows are valued for crossbreeding to pass on their famed maternal qualities. They have proved heat tolerant and resistant to ticks, and are crossed with zebu in southern Africa.

Related Breeds

The Gelbray beef breed of the US resulted from mating Gelbvieh bulls with Brahman cows. Also from North America comes the Balancer, a trademarked hybrid: 25–75 per cent Gelbvieh and 25–75 per cent Angus or Red Angus.

Size

Bull weight .... 1000–1300 kg (2400–2900 lb)

Cow weight .... 650–850 kg (1400–1850 lb)

Origin & Distribution

Gelbvieh cows originated from Bavaria, in Germany, and have spread to North America, the UK, Australia, South Africa, Namibia, Zimbabwe, Brazil and some European countries.

Bavaria, Germany

BELGIAN BLUE
3-YEAR-OLD COW

The BELGIAN BLUE's 'double muscling' gives the bull the look of a prize body-builder, its beefy shoulders and back end bulging with meaty muscle. The muscling can cause calving problems in purebreds, which often need a caesarean section. The Belgian Blue, or White Blue, evolved when imported Durham Shorthorn and Dutch Black Pied bulls were used to improve local red-pied Belgian herds in the 19th century.

Features

This placid, large but fine-boned breed is long in the body and its hips are hidden under those rounded muscular hindquarters – roundness is a general characteristic. The coat colour is often white with a scattering of blue patches but also ranges from white through blue roan to blue. The horns are short.

Use

Originally used for milk as well as meat, the Belgian Blue has been developed since the 1960s essentially as a producer of large quantities of lean, tender low-cholesterol meat. In most countries it is used as a sire for crossbred beef calves.

Related Breeds

To avoid calving problems and suit local needs, different countries have created their own types of less extreme Belgian Blue, such as the Bleue du Nord in France, the Danish Blue and White and the British Blue. Another double-muscled breed is the Piedmontese.

Size

Bull weight .... 900–1200 kg (1990–2650 lb)

Cow weight .... 700–850 kg (1550–1875 lb)

Origin & Distribution

The breed originated in Belgium's Walloon region. Imported into the UK and North America in the 1980s, it is now widely found in Australia, New Zealand, Europe and Japan.

Walloon, Belgium

RED ANGUS
1-YEAR-OLD HEIFER

In cow genetics, most black breeds carry recessive red genes, but those who want a black breed would not breed from red cows. When the Aberdeen-Angus of Scotland was selected in the 19th century for black as the breed colour, red calves continued to be born and registered but became unfashionable and dwindled. In 1954 some innovative breeders, proud of the RED ANGUS, created the Red Angus Association of America.

Features

Red Angus cows look like black Aberdeen-Angus or American Angus cows except that their coats are dark to golden red. They are naturally polled. Performance qualities like quick growth and carcass quality are more important to breeders than appearance.

Use

In some countries, red cattle are preferred to black, which is where the Red Angus comes into its own. Like black Angus cattle, it is one of the world's producers of top-class quality meat. The Reds are often used to beef up other breeds without turning them black. Many breeders find that the Red is more heat tolerant than its black relative.

Related Breeds

The Red Angus has been used to create the Red Brangus (with Brahman), Regus, Cuprem Hybrid and Hash Cross in North America, as well as introduce the polled factor into the Santa Gertrudis, Droughtmaster, Brahman, Hereford and old red European breeds.

Size

Bull weight .... 815–1000 kg (1800–2200 lb)

Cow weight .... 500–590 kg (1100–1300 lb)

Origin & Distribution

The breed originated in Scotland, but was first registered separately from the black Angus in the US. It is a separate breed in the US, Canada, the UK, Australia, Brazil and South Africa.

Scotland

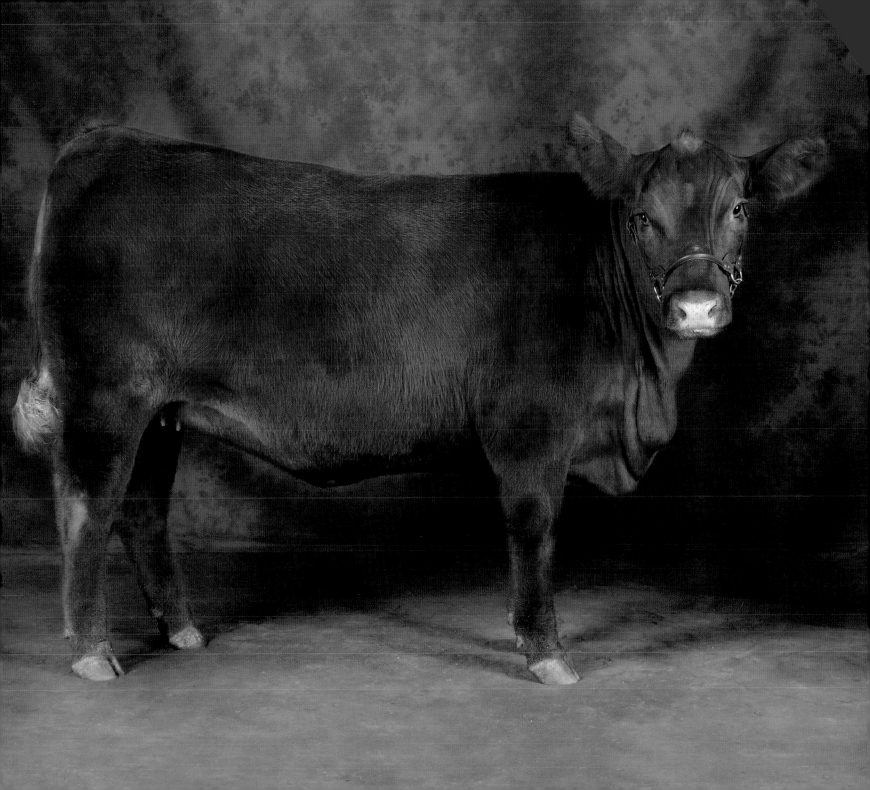

BRAHMOUSIN

1-YEAR-OLD HEIFER

The BRAHMOUSIN is a combination of the humped subtropical Brahman with the temperate French Limousin to get the best of two continents. In the 1970s Daryl Wiggins, of Texas, received embryos from a Limousin cow called Gloria. He began a crossbreeding programme with Brahman cattle which led to a mixture that was ultimately five-eighths Limousin and three-eighths Brahman.

Features

Signs of a loose dewlap and largish ears are the main zebu features seen in Brahmousins. Bulls have a bit of a hump but it is barely discernible in the cows. The coat reflects Limousin ancestry: it is usually golden red to tan, with lighter areas underneath and around the eyes and muzzle. The horns are short.

Use

This is a beef composite and the Brahman/Limousin combination means good tolerance of heat and insects and a long breeding life on the one side, with beefiness, lean meat and good growth rates on the other. Brahmousin cows are milky mothers. The proportions are not fixed in the breed; those wanting Brahmousin cows for northern areas would increase the Limousin percentage.

Related Breeds

The Brahmousin is one of several breeds developed in the US by crossing Brahman zebus with European cattle. It is broadly similar to the Bravado, but the latter is always polled.

Size

Bull weight .... 815–900 kg (1800–2000 lb)

Cow weight .... 545–590 kg (1200–1300 lb)

Origin & Distribution

Originating in Texas, the Brahmousin is found in other southern states and also in Australia and Canada.

Texas, US

BRAVADO

2-YEAR-OLD HEIFER

Like the Brahmousin, this breed combines the French Limousin with the humped Brahman. Breeding started in 1970 at the Rottmann Ranch, Oklahoma, with imports of Polled Limousin from Canada. In 1986 a polled Limousin cow was mated with a Red Brahman bull, and their calf, Diablo, became the father of the BRAVADO breed. All full-blood Bravados trace back to the ranch's original Polled Limousin stock.

Features

Purebred Bravados are solid red or black (no white allowed), with dark skin pigmentation, and above all polled. The colour range includes for preference 'Bravado' (red with dark nose, eyes and hooves) or solid black; also mahogany or caramel.The horizontal ears are a selected feature of the breed and are between the large droop of the Brahman and the usual European size and carriage.

Use

Like other Brahman crosses, the Bravado is a beef breed that does particularly well in hotter climates. Bravado cows calve easily and milk well in suckler herds and are said to be 'fescue friendly'.

Related Breeds

With their similar origins from a combination of Brahman and Limousin, Bravado and Brahmousin cows differ mainly in the polled factor, uniformity and colour standards bred into the Bravado but not into the Brahmousin. The Bravado breeds true; the Brahmousin is less standardised.

Size

Bull weight .... 815–950 kg (1800–2100 lb)

Cow weight .... 500–545 kg (1100–1200 lb)

Origin & Distribution

The breed was developed in Miami, Oklahoma, and has spread to other parts of the US.

Oklahoma, US

BRITISH BLONDE
5-YEAR-OLD COW

The BRITISH BLONDE is a national version of France's Blonde d'Aquitaine. The latter was created by the French government in 1961–2 by combining several old yellowy-brown Pyrenean mountain breeds under one umbrella, like the cart-pulling Garonnais, the pale milk-and-meat Villard de Lans and the Pyrenean Blond. The new combination went international in the early 1970s.

Features

The Blonde's short coat is often described as corn-coloured and the shade varies from light to dark, with paler areas around the eyes, muzzle, underbelly and inner thighs. The skin is quite thick and the body is long. The triangular face is quite long from poll to muzzle; the horns are thick and short and some animals are polled.

Use

This low-maintenance high-yielding beef breed has benefited from a rigorous breeding and evaluation programme in France since its inception in the 1960s. Both pure and crossbred newborn Blonde calves are small, slim and fine-boned, making for easier calving, but then they grow fast from about two weeks old. The breed does well in hot, humid climates as well as in cold.

Related Breeds

The Blonde d'Aquitaine absorbed the Pyrenean Blond, itself a rare group including blond Béarnais, chestnut Aure et Saint-Girons and white Lourdais cows. Like Britain, several other countries have their own national Blonde.

Size

Bull weight .... 770–1040 kg (1700–2300 lb)

Cow weight .... 500–680 kg (1100–1500 lb)

Origin & Distribution

The Blonde originated in southwest France and has spread to North America, Australia, New Zealand, the UK, other parts of Europe, including Denmark, Sweden, the Netherlands and Ireland.

southwest France

BRITISH BLUE
6-YEAR-OLD COW

British breeders began to import the double-muscled Belgian Blue in 1982 and set to work to create a type more suited to British markets and farming methods. Above all, they wanted to reduce the breed's notorious calving difficulties and to breed an animal whose muscling was not extreme. They achieved these aims with the BRITISH BLUE by the end of the 1990s.

Features

British Blues are muscular but not to the extreme of the Belgian Blue. They are large, with long bodies, a rounded rump and well-padded hips. Coat colour ranges from white to black; markings are either blue roan or black-and-white pied.

Use

The British Blue is wholeheartedly a beef breed and is popular as a terminal sire used on dairy cattle to beef up their calves, as well as on suckler cows of various breeds. The meat from British Blues, whether pure or crossbred, is very lean. Most British Blue cows now calve 'naturally', helped by reduced muscling and also a shorter gestation period, so that the calf's birth weight is lower.

Related Breeds

The British Blue's immediate ancestor, the Belgian Blue, had plenty of Shorthorn blood. Several countries other than the UK also now have their own 'national' Blues.

Size

Bull weight .... 860–1300 kg (1900–2800 lb)

Cow weight .... 500–840 kg (1500–1850 lb)

Origin & Distribution

Central and southern Belgium were the breed's original homes before it came to the UK in 1982. The British Blue is now also popular in Australia, New Zealand and Chile.

Belgium

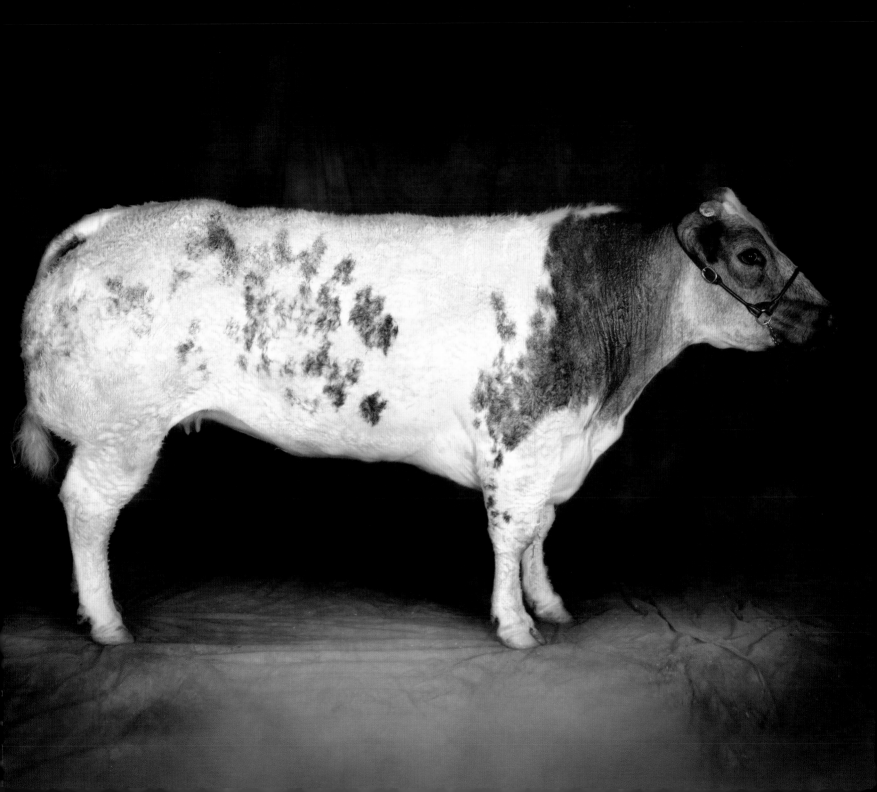

MAINETAINER
2-YEAR-OLD COW

The MaineTainer is more a trademark than a breed, created by the American Maine-Anjou Association in 2002 to describe registered animals that are a quarter to five-eighths Maine-Anjou. The Maine-Anjou itself was created when the Count de Falloux imported Durham Shorthorns in the 1830s and crossed them with his local dual-purpose Mancelle cows in northwest France.

Features

MaineTainers are often black, depending on other breeds in the mix. The original Maine-Anjou cows are big and distinctive: their Shorthorn ancestry is reflected in the coat colours of red, roan or red-and-white – usually dark red with small white patches on the head, belly, hind legs and tail. In North America, many Maine-Anjou cows are now solid black due to deliberate crossbreeding with Angus. Their horns are short, but increasingly they are polled.

Use

The Maine-Anjou still plays a dual-purpose role as a milk-and-meat breed in several countries. In France, many smaller farms milk half their herd and let the other cows each rear a pair of calves for beef. In the US, Maine-Anjous are bred for beef.

Related Breeds

A recently-developed composite breed is the Brah-Maine, which is a combination of five-eighths Maine-Anjou and three-eighths Brahman zebu. A Brah-Maine breed society was established in 1985.

Size

Bull weight .... 900–1400 kg (2000–3100 lb)

Cow weight .... 635–860 kg (1400–1900 lb)

Origin & Distribution

The MaineTainer is a US hybrid from the Maine-Anjou of northwest France. The Maine-Anjou has spread to North America, the UK, Australia, New Zealand, Russia and parts of Europe.

northwest France

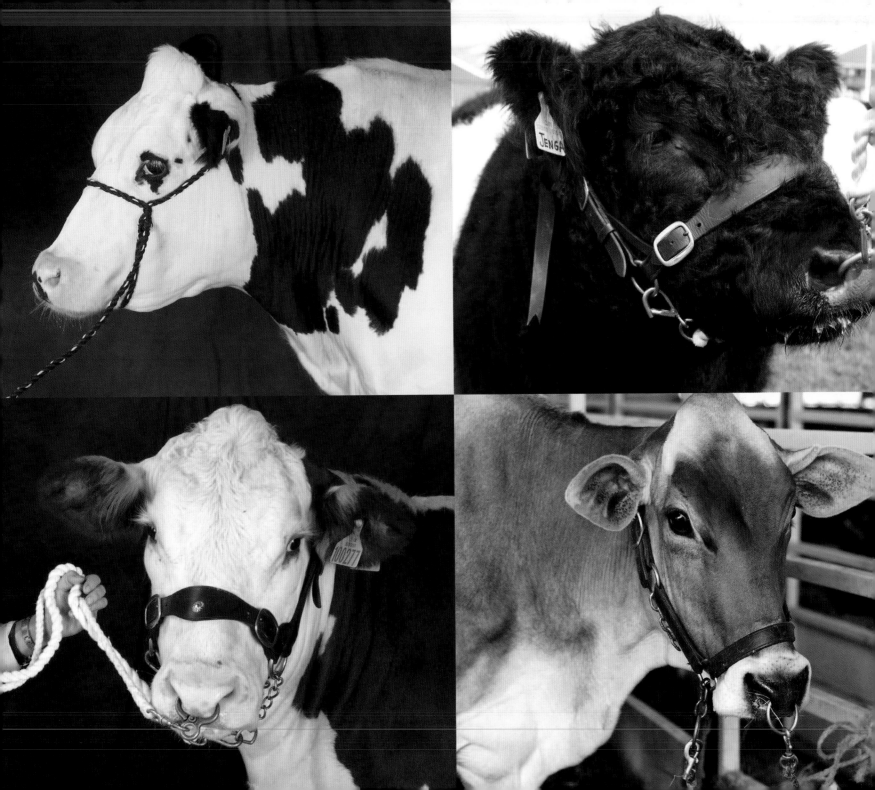

REPORTAGE

Don't be misled by the TRANQUIL expressions of our *bovine* models: behind the scenes at the shows, things are just as *frantic* as at any COUTURE outing. Once in front of an audience, however, these *serene* hoofers know how to STRUT their stuff – and they have the *rosettes* to show for it.

The Tulsa
State Fair,
Oklahoma, US

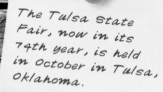

The Tulsa State
Fair, now in its
74th year, is held
in October in Tulsa,
Oklahoma.

a contemplative moment
backstage.

Taking the bull by the horns.

The Tulsa
State Fair,
Oklahoma, US

an opportunity to meet
and greet.

The Tulsa State
Fair welcomes
competitors
of all ages.

What are you looking at, punk?

The South of England Show, Sussex, UK

After the excitement: a moment of ennui backstage.

Making cow's eyes at the camera.

The South of England Show attracts over 90,000 visitors from across Europe every year.

Remember, it's the taking part that counts.

The South of England Show, Sussex, UK

Never too young to start – showing a calf the ropes.

say cheese!

The key to success is attention to detail at both ends.

Preened, primped, polished and ready for action.

The South of England Show is hosted by the South of England Agricultural Society every year in June in Ardingly, West Sussex.

Lending a helping hoof.

The Royal
Show,
Stoneleigh,
UK

Smooth as silk: the glamorous
product of hours of grooming.

Not a wise move — she
may lose patience.

Ready for her close-up —
stepping out into the limelight.

Slightly baffled.
It's a long day and
a lot of demands
when it's your
first time.

More than 114,000
people attended the
last ever Royal Show
which took place in
July 2009.

The Royal
Show,
Stoneleigh,
UK

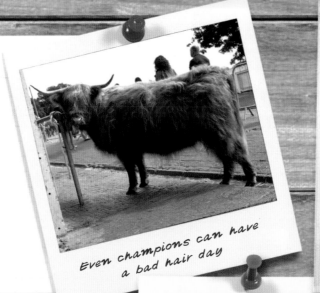
Even champions can have
a bad hair day

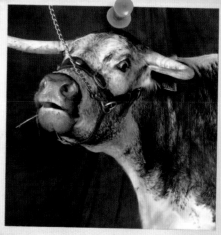
Not at all sure! Lead gently
and stay well out of the way
of those impressive horns.

It's all for a good
cause.

Since the Royal
Show began in
1839, there have
been 159 Shows.

However much grooming
they're given, some styles
just stay windswept.

GLOSSARY

Aurochs wild ancestor (*Bos primigenius*) of domesticated cattle

Beef breed cattle bred to produce meat

Belted a coat pattern with white band around the middle

Blocking trimming the coat to draw attention away from minor faults or accentuate good points, e.g. clipping hair along the back to make a straight top line

Breed an isolated population specifically bred as a unique genetic type that is externally recognisable as a member of that breed and will 'breed true', i.e. the offspring will be similarly recognisable

Brindle coat colour streaked with another colour

Butterfat fat globules in the milk (used for cream and butter making)

Colour-marking ability of a bull to pass his coat colour and markings on to all his offspring

Colour-pointed a coat pattern in which the main colour is white but the points (e.g. muzzle, ears, tail switch) are coloured

Crest a slight hump in bulls of taurine breeds

Criollo cattle of Spanish origin in Latin America

Crossbreeding mating between a bull of one breed and a cow of another

Dairy breed one bred to produce milk

Dewlap loose skin under the throat

Disbudding removal of horn 'buds' in a young calf to prevent horn growth

Double muscling extreme musculature seen particularly in the Belgian Blue

Draught animal one whose role is to pull agricultural implements, carts etc. (some are ridden or act as pack animals)

Dual-purpose bred to combine the roles of milk production and beef

Finchback a coat pattern with a white line along the back and over the tail

Heifer a cow that has not yet had a calf

Herdbook a register of pedigree animals kept by a breed society

Hump in zebu, fatty mass perched above the shoulders and chest; in sanga the hump is smaller and more muscular and sits further forward

Hybrid offspring from two different species; also sometimes used to describe 'synthetic breeds'

Inbreeding mating animals that are closely related to each other

Oxen draught cattle, usually castrated males

Pied a coat pattern in which the colour is broken up with defined white patches

Poll a hard lateral ridge on top of the head from which horns would grow in a horned breed

Polled naturally hornless (genetically unable to grow horns). Horned breeds are disbudded as calves.

Purebred offspring of two animals of the same breed

Roan a coat colour in which hairs of two or more different colours are mingled, giving a fuzzy effect

Sanga a type of cattle in southern Africa with small or vestigial muscular cervico-thoracic hump

Scurs degenerate horns (loose etc.) sometimes seen in polled cattle if not purebred

Suckler cow a cow that rears calves (hers or adopted) on her own milk

Switch a tassel of coarse hair at the tail's end

Synthetic an experimental mixture of breeds

Taurine humpless cattle, in contrast to sanga and zebu, and typical of European breeds

Zebu a type of cattle, originally Asian, with a fatty thoracic hump

SHOWS & ORGANISATIONS

The following is a list of major agricultural and livestock shows and breed societies:

UK SHOWS

DEVON COUNTY SHOW
www.devoncountyshow.co.uk

EAST OF ENGLAND SHOW
www.eastofengland.org.uk

GREAT YORKSHIRE SHOW
www.yas.co.uk

KENT COUNTY SHOW
www.kentshowground.co.uk

MONMOUTH SHOW
www.monmouthshow.co.uk

NEW FOREST SHOW
www.newforestshow.co.uk

NEWPORT SHOW
www.newportshow.org

RARE BREEDS SHOW, SINGLETON
www.wealddown.co.uk

ROYAL BATH & WEST SHOW
www.bathandwest.com

ROYAL CORNWALL SHOW
www.royalcornwallshow.org

ROYAL HIGHLAND SHOW
www.royalhighlandshow.org

ROYAL NORFOLK SHOW
www.royalnorfolkshow.co.uk

ROYAL SHOW
www.royalshow.org.uk

ROYAL WELSH SHOW
www.rwas.co.uk

SOUTH OF ENGLAND SHOW
www.seas.org.uk

STITHIANS SHOW
www.stithiansshow.org.uk

NORTH AMERICAN SHOWS

AMERICAN ROYAL LIVESTOCK SHOW (KANSAS CITY, MISSOURI)
www.americanroyal.com

HOUSTON LIVESTOCK SHOW (TEXAS)
www.hlsr.com

NATIONAL WESTERN STOCK SHOW (DENVER, COLORADO)
www.nationalwestern.com

NORTH AMERICAN INTERNATIONAL LIVESTOCK EXPOSITION (LOUISVILLE, KENTUCKY)
www.livestockexpo.org

ROYAL AGRICULTURAL WINTER FAIR (TORONTO, CANADA)
www.royalfair.org

SOUTHWESTERN EXPOSITION & LIVESTOCK SHOW (FORT WORTH, TEXAS)
www.fwssr.com

ORGANISATIONS

AMERICAN LIVESTOCK BREEDS CONSERVANCY (ALBC)
www.albc-usa.org

CENTRE FOR DAIRY INFORMATION (FOR BRITISH DAIRY BREED SOCIETIES)
www.ukcows.com/theCDI

NATIONAL BEEF ASSOCIATION (FOR BRITISH BEEF BREED SOCIETIES)
www.nationalbeefassociation.com

RARE BREEDS SURVIVAL TRUST (RBST)
www.rbst.org.uk

ROYAL AGRICULTURAL SOCIETY OF ENGLAND (RASE)
www.rase.org.uk

BREED SOCIETIES

Several British breed societies are based at the National Agricultural Centre, Stoneleigh Park, Kenilworth, Warwickshire (for a useful list, go to www.stoneleighpark.com), including those for Beef Shorthorn, Dairy Shorthorn, British Blonde, British Charolais, British Limousin, British Simmental and Murray Grey. Most of the dairy breeds (Guernsey, Holstein, Jersey) have their societies at Scotsbridge House, Scots Hill, Rickmansworth, Hertfordshire.

OTHER BREED SOCIETY WEBSITES:

Aberdeen-Angus: www.aberdeen-angus.co.uk

Ankole-Watusi: www.awir.org and www.watusicattle.com

Ayrshire: www.ayrshirescs.org

Belgian Blue: www.belgianblue.co.uk (UK) or www.belgianblue.org (US)

Belted Galloway: www.beltedgalloways.co.uk

Brahman: www.brahman.org

Brahmousin: www.americanbrahmousincouncil.org

Braunvieh: www.braunvieh.org

Bravado: www.bravadocattle.com

British Blonde: www.britishblondesociety.co.uk

British Blue: www.britishbluecattle.org

British White: www.britishwhitecattle.co.uk

Brown Swiss: www.brownswiss.org (UK) or www.brownswissusa.com (US)

Charolais: www.charolais.co.uk

Devon: www.redrubydevon.co.uk

Dexter: www.dextercattle.co.uk (UK) or www.purebreddextercattle.org (US)

Galloway: www.gallowaycattlesociety.co.uk

Gelbvieh: www.gelbviehworld.com

Gloucester: www.gloucestercattle.org.uk

Guernsey: www.guernseycattle.com (England) or www.worldguernseys.org

Hereford: www.herefordcattle.org or www.thcbc.co.uk (traditional type)

Highland: www.highlandcattlesociety.com

Holstein: www.holstein-uk.org (UK) or www.holsteinusa.com (US)

Jersey: www.ukjerseys.com (UK) or www.usjersey.com (US)

Limousin: www.limousin.co.uk

Lincoln Red: www.lincolnredcattlesociety.co.uk

Longhorn: www.longhorncattlesociety.com

MaineTainer: www.maine-anjou.org (US)

Red Angus: www.redangus.org (US)

Red Poll: www.redpoll.org

Salers: www.salers-cattle-society.co.uk

Santa Gertrudis: www.santagertrudis.org

Shorthorn: www.shorthorn.co.uk

Simmental: www.britishsimmental.co.uk

South Devon: www.sdhbs.org.uk

Sussex: www.sussexcattlesociety.org.uk

Texas Longhorn: www.tlbaa.org

Welsh Black: www.welshblackcattlesociety.com

ACKNOWLEDGMENTS

We would like to thank the organisations below for their help and cooperation in arranging the photo shoots at the agricultural shows.

Special thanks to: Susan Fleet, Steve Cook, Jo Illsley, Brandi Herndon, Kara Eschbah and Josh New.

South of England Show
www.seas.org.uk

The Royal Show
www.royalshow.org.uk

Tulsa State Fair
www.exposquare.com

We would also like to thanks all the cow owners and breeders for their time and assistance at the photo shoots.:

Ankole Watusi Vernon P. Base
Braunvieh Albert & Joan Thorne
Highland Mrs S. Tedbury
Gloucester William & Janet Murphy
Devon Jeff & Pat Thomas
South Devon Daniel & Laura Cook
Sussex Jo Masters
Salers Carolyn Fox
Limousin Buriton Estate Ltd, Handler Mary Reynolds
Charolais Mortimers Farm
Simmental Roger Birch
Texas Longhorn John & Diann Chase
Jersey Mrs Pam Ainslie
Guernsey Tyler Chupp, Chupps Guernsey Farm
Aberdeen-Angus Angus Stovold
Ayrshire Oathall Community College

Belted Galloway Whitepool Belted Galloways
Hereford Carolyn Fletcher
Longhorn P. V. Robinson
Dairy Shorthorn Randy Wright
Beef Shorthorn D. Mellish
Lincoln Red H. M. & J. M. Needler
British White New Biddenden Green Farm
Red Poll Terry & Helen Mancey
Dexter Mrs Henderson
Welsh Black Charlotte Reynolds
Brahman Rich Cattle Co.
Santa Gertrudis Shane Broussard
Holstein M-6 Diary Farm, LLC
Brown Swiss The Dean Family
Gelbvieh Shannon Worrell
Belgian Blue Ronnie & Kathy Price
Red Angus Tony & Carla Clark
Brahmousin Hilltop Farms
Bravado Ron Rottmann
British Blonde Ian & Sue Archer
British Blue James Barber
MaineTainer Diamonds In The Rough Cattle Co. (Blakley Family)

Picture credits
Corbis/Sandro Vannini: 8
Alamy/Arco Images GmbH: 9
Corbis/Brian A. Vikander: 11
Corbis/Yann Arthus-Bertrand: 12
Corbis/Jamil Bittar: 13
Museum of English Rural Life, University of Reading: 14.

INDEX

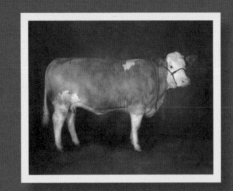

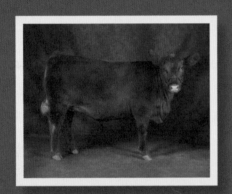